The Authorities

~ *Powerful Wisdom from Leaders in the Field* ~

TONY DEBOGORSKI
Award Winning Author

AuthoritiesPress

Publisher
Authorities Press
Markham, ON
Canada

Printed in the United States.

FOREWORD

Experts are to be admired for their knowledge, but they often remain unrecognized by the general public because they save their information and insights for paying customers and clients. There are many experts in a given field, but their impact is limited to the handful of people with whom they work.

Unlike experts, authorities share their knowledge and expertise far more broadly, so they make a big impact on the world. Authorities become known and admired as leading experts and, as such, typically do very well economically and professionally. Most authorities are also mature enough to know that part of the joy of monetary success is the accompanying moral and spiritual obligation to give back.

Many people want to learn and work with well-respected and generous authorities, but don't always know where to find them. They may be known to their peers, or within a specific community, but have not had the opportunity to reach a wider audience. At one time, they might have submitted a proposal to the For Dummies or Chicken Soup for the Soul series of books, but it's now almost impossible to get accepted as a new author in such branded book series.

It is more than fitting that Raymond Aaron, an internationally known and respected authority in his own right, would be the one to recognize the need for a new venue in which authorities could share their considerable knowledge with readers everywhere. As the only author ever to be included in both of the book series mentioned above, Raymond has had the opportunity to give back and he understands how crucial it is for authorities to have a platform from which to share their expertise.

I have known and worked with Raymond for a number of years and consider him a valued friend and talented coach. He knows how to spot talented and knowledgeable people and he desires to see them prosper. Over the years, success coaching and speaking engagements around the world have made it possible for Raymond to meet many of these talented authorities. He recognizes and relates to their passion and enthusiasm for what they do, as well as their desire to share what they know. He tells me that's why he created this new nonfiction branded book series, The Authorities.

Dr. Nido Qubein
President, High Point University

TABLE OF CONTENTS

INTRODUCTION

This book introduces you to *The Authorities* — individuals who have distinguished themselves in life and in business. Authorities make a big impact on the world. Authorities are leaders in their chosen fields. Authorities typically do very well financially, and are evolved enough to know that part of the joy of monetary success is the accompanying social, moral and spiritual obligation to give back.

Authorities are not just outstanding. They are also *known* to be outstanding.

This additional element begins to explain the difference between two strategic business and life concepts — one that seems great, but isn't, and the other that fills in the essential missing gap of the first.

The first concept is "the expert."

What is an expert? The real definition is …

EXPERT: *a person who knows stuff*

People who have attained a very senior academic degree (like a PhD or an MD) definitely know stuff. People who read voraciously and retain what they read definitely know stuff. Unfortunately, just because you know stuff does not mean that anyone respects the fact that you do. Even though some experts are successful, alas, most are not — because knowing stuff is not enough.

Well, then, what is the missing piece?

What the expert lacks, "the authority" has. The authority both knows stuff and is *known* to know stuff. So, more simply …

AUTHORITY: *a person who is known as an expert*

The difference is not subtle. The difference is not merely semantic. The difference is enormous.

When it comes to this subject, there are actually three categories in which people fall:

- People who don't know much and are unsuccessful in life and in business. Most people fall in this category.

- People who know stuff, but still don't leave much of a footprint in the world. There are a lot of people like this.

- Experts who are also *known* as experts become authorities and authorities are always wondrously successful. Authorities are able to contribute more to humanity through both their chosen work and their giving back.

You will definitely know some of *The Authorities* in this book, especially since there are some world-famous ones. Others are just as exceptional, but you may not yet know about them. Our featured author is Tony Debogorski.

The reality is, change is a part of life, whether we want to accept it or not. In *What Does Change Mean to You?*, Tony Debogorski explores how change can be a force for good in your life and how you can benefit from it. Right from the start, he acknowledges that there are two types of change, the ones that happen due to circumstances and the ones that we initiate.

Throughout *What Does Change Mean to You?*, Tony also shares five key elements to create the right mindset for embracing change and helping you end a fear of change. It is an exciting time in the world, with technology bringing us ever closer. As you take this journey with Tony, you can give yourself the skills needed to joyfully accept change and use it to help you grow, explore, and imagine!

Fear of the unknown can leave you unable to accept or initiate real change in your life. Tony Debogorski takes you through the keys to not only accept change, but to thrive in the face of change in your life.

As Tony shares his own journey, he also demonstrates how change can enrich your life, both in terms of experiences and the people you meet. By demonstrating the importance of an open mind, Tony shares one of the critical aspects of embracing change in all areas of your life. Throughout this chapter, Tony also shares various lessons he has learned, while recognizing that whether a change is negative or not largely depends on our viewpoint.

Opening your mind and life to change involves more than just a willingness to listen. It means being active in embracing the benefits of change, not only in your life, but the lives of others. Use this book as a guide to help you take the next step in embracing and becoming an advocate for change!

They are *The Authorities*. Learn from them. Connect with them. Let them uplift you. Learning from them and working with them is the secret ingredient for success which may well allow you to rise to the level of Authority soon.

To be considered for inclusion in a subsequent edition of *The Authorities,* register to attend a future event at www.aaron.com/events where you will be interviewed and considered.

What Does Change Mean to You?

Fundamental Elements for a Vibrant, Fulfilling Life

TONY DEBOGORSKI

How do you view change? For many individuals, change has become something to fear. It invokes feelings of anxiety and potential loss. There is often little focus on what we can gain from change. Instead, the negative feelings and thought patterns overwhelm us, which can make change more difficult to accept and benefit from.

Think of the flight or fight response. Change, if we don't manage it effectively, can trigger that response. It can make us respond as if our lives are being threatened, when it's more likely that we are simply being affected by changing circumstances. Some of these circumstances are in our control and others are out of our control. However, if we can alter our reaction to change, then we can reap some amazing benefits.

Yes, you can benefit from change. However, in order to do so you need to be willing to create a new mindset in regards to how you view change and how you choose to act. Without the right mindset, you might be missing out on a change that could give depth to your life and the lives of those around you.

Changes, both those that happen to us and the ones that we create ourselves, have the potential to create new opportunities and experiences we might otherwise miss. These can give us another perspective and enrich our lives. Change did just that for me as a young man.

I grew up in rural Canada, where hard work and sweat were the building blocks of your success. I learned to be a jack of all trades, because that was the way you got things done around a farm. When I left to attend university, the idea was that I would end up coming home, marrying my high school girlfriend, and raising my family in the farming community where I was raised.

This step towards a university education was already a big change, since only a few of my family members actually went on to get a university education. Working hard was our way of life, and it was hard physical work. I couldn't imagine any other way, but university gave me a new way to live and introduced me to the idea of working smarter, not harder.

My life was enriched by not only the classes I attended, but the people

I met. I was exposed to those who hadn't lived their entire life on a farm. I was exposed to different perspectives on how to tackle a variety of challenges. It altered my perception of the world, giving me a broader viewpoint. At the same time, I also deepened my appreciation of the values my parents instilled in me.

It was my first experience with change, but definitely not my last. I took the step to open my mind to change, which allowed me to get comfortable with the idea. During this time, I learned that it was okay to find assistance in accepting a change and acting on it without fear. The life I live today is defined by change. Now, instead of fear and anxiety, I welcome change for the blessings it may bring. How did I get to this point? It started with my willingness to learn and grew from there.

There is a process to change, but if we are not careful, we can actually prolong the process and make it more difficult. Let's walk through the reality of change. First, you have the old status quo. This is the reality of how things are right now. It could be a fairly peaceful way of life or you could find it difficult, but it is what you know.

Now a foreign element is introduced. It could be a new job or a move, for example. Most of the time, our first reaction is to resist, fearing the chaos that we are sure is to follow. After a point, we see the transforming idea of change and begin to integrate it into our lives. As time goes on, we then integrate the change into our lives and thus create a new status quo. Still, the impact of many aspects of this process can be lessened if we take a different point of view toward change.

Through mentors and my own experiences, I learned the key elements that can impact your ability to not only weather change, but thrive in the process. These five key elements are necessary to create the right mindset, one that embraces change, instead of being governed by a fear of change.

KEY #1. SELF-BELIEF

The first key is your belief in yourself. This is the foundation of a vibrant and fulfilling life. Without confidence in your own ability to handle challenges, you will see change as a crisis, instead of a benefit or an opportunity to grow as an individual.

Throughout our lives, we are told how to act, dress, and even think. Our belief systems are influenced by this training. In addition, as we grow older and other influences come into play from the world around us. Just take a moment and think about all the people and ideas you encounter on a daily basis. These could be teachers, family members, workmates, television, the internet, etc. The list goes on and on.

All of these influences are not focused on teaching us to think for ourselves, but instead are focused on developing our thinking to fall in line with who they believe we should be. Call it the social conditioning of our world. There often isn't time to learn who we are, to spend time with ourselves, to think, imagine, and explore the world. Instead, if we don't buy out the time, we can find that we are dissatisfied with our lives and unable to determine why.

We often have our purpose in life defined for us by others. This can lead to a lack of fulfillment in our lives, especially if what we are supposed to be doesn't fit our true vision of who we are.

The key is to stop and examine your belief system. Focus on your values. How many of them would you say you genuinely believe and how many have you taken on because of someone else in your life? It is amazing how many of our beliefs may no longer be serving us, but we are still using them to define ourselves and the world around us. Like the traditional fall and spring cleaning of our homes, we need to constantly be willing to clean the beliefs that no longer serve us or contribute to the growth and happiness of our lives from our consciousness.

Do you wake up in the morning satisfied with where you are in life? Can you look in the mirror and see a face excited to meet the day? Do you feel accountable for your life or does it feel as if your life is happening to you? How you see the world is based on your self-belief. What crafts your self-belief?

It hinges on your ability to see yourself master a skill and then be able to do it again and again successfully. Positive experiences help us grow our confidence in ourselves and define who we are. These moments often start in our early childhood, setting up a pattern throughout our lives.

My first memory of confidence building occurred when I was 11 years old. The regional elementary track and field meet was coming up. I wanted to win the top male athlete award. Although I had participated in the meet in the past, I hadn't won before. This time, I decided to do things differently. In preparation for the meet, I spent extra time training, including running after school. I was determined and my goal dominated my thoughts. It was a type of visualization, one that helped build my confidence going into the meet.

I had entered into five events and there were points for coming into first, second, and third place. On the day of the meet, it was sunny, the field and track were dry. Conditions were perfect for this outdoor event. My focus was on doing my best to earn the most points possible. At the end of the event, I had four first place ribbons and one for second place. I was presented with the trophy for top male athlete. That feeling of accomplishment boosted my sense of what I could do and built my self-belief.

What goals have you set that you were able to accomplish on your own? How did you feel after you achieved your goal? Setting and accomplishing goals is a great way to feel better about yourself. How does this translate into having a different mindset about change? When you feel confidence in your abilities, you will not find yourself fearing change and the challenges it can present.

However, in the midst of a major change, you might find yourself neglecting your needs. How often do we put ourselves last when others around us are in need of our time and attention? While we might think that it will last for only a short period of time, putting ourselves on the back burner can become a routine, one that has a negative impact on our lives.

This can leave you worn out mentally and put you into a negative frame of mind. I can point to research and personal experiences to give you examples of why a negative mindset can be the anti-change and can encourage you to avoid thinking about the potential benefits of change.

Once you focus on caring for your needs, you are in a better position to weather change and give assistance to others. Once you find confidence and strength in yourself and your abilities, you will be able to master whatever change and challenges come your way.

One important point is that you might still be afraid, but don't let it paralyze you into not acting at all. Remember those moments of success and allow them to motivate you to keep going. The keys to being self-reliant are perseverance, dedication, and integrity. When you have them, you will be able to conquer just about anything.

KEY #2. PURPOSE

Your life is a journey and you are the navigator. Some individuals choose to navigate based on their surroundings, essentially letting the waves aimlessly lead them along. In the end, that kind of life rarely leads to happiness with change or with yourself. You become a product of your circumstances, instead of defining yourself on your own terms.

What is purpose? According to the American Heritage Dictionary, it is "The object toward which one strives or for which something exists, an aim or a goal. The reason for which anything is done, created or exists, an aim or a goal."

When you examine your own life, are you excited about what you do? Could you define the purpose of your life? For some, their purpose becomes apparent when they are young. They find the passion that defines their lives and shapes their careers. Others never find that purpose, leaving them to struggle to find satisfaction with their lives.

If you haven't defined the purpose of your life, then it is time to think about what you enjoy. What sparks your passion? What gets you excited to get out of bed in the morning? Once you start to define your purpose, set your goals around what you enjoy. This can help you gain perspective on your purpose.

However, keep in mind that your purpose is not set in stone. It can change over time as you gain life experience and a better understanding of yourself. Taking action will help you be drawn to what you like. Try new things. Consider the spiritual influences in your life. To postulate is the act of creation. It can happen when you think, write, or speak something into being. Focus, because if you think it, then you can do it.

Change can be initiated by you. It doesn't have to be dominated by circumstances outside of your control. You can start by taking one action that will move you closer to a specific goal. That goal could be to simply change your way of thinking or to release a belief that is no longer serving you, but could be limiting you instead.

With your purpose defined, you could move forward to produce the life you want and mindset for change, which starts with how you take care of yourself.

KEY #3. HEALTH

Fear and anxiety can have physical repercussions. They impact how our bodies feel, as well as our ability to fight off illnesses and deal with chronic conditions. Research has proven time and again that our minds can influence our physical well-being.

Are you poisoning your body through the negative thoughts you are dwelling on? To create the energy necessary for a vibrant fulfilling life you need to maximize your mental state, maintain your physical body, and nourish yourself properly. Keep your mind focused on what is possible, instead of focusing on what can't be done or any potentially negative consequences.

The combination of your mind and body is a synergistic relationship. It means you need to take care of both to achieve overall well-being. To start, let's focus on your physical body. Are you getting out on a regular basis to exercise and stretch your muscles? Do you raise your heart rate? One of the interesting side effects of physical activity is how it can impact our mood. When we are uplifted in mood, it translates into our thought processes. Regular physical exercise can contribute to greater overall positivity in our lives.

If you find it hard to get out on your own and get physically active, then consider finding a support group, a partner, or even a gym where you can be held accountable for showing up and putting in the effort. You will appreciate the results in terms of your health, making it worth the effort. Additionally, the physical benefits will allow you to grow in other areas of your life, thus making change more welcome, especially as your body grows stronger.

When it comes to your physical well-being, the reality is that you are what you put into your body. If you don't fuel your body for optimal performance, then it can't give you the very best physically. That can have a domino effect on how you operate mentally. When you are tired and not feeling your best, can you honestly say that you have made your best decisions? Or do you find yourself rethinking those choices at a later date?

There are five products, which I refer to as the five white poisons, that you need to be aware of. They can be found in a variety of foods throughout your local grocery store. So much of what we eat today has been processed extensively, removing the natural nutrients and fiber-rich parts. As a result, we are exposed to more of these five products than ever before. What are these five white poisons? Sugar, starch, flour, salt, and milk.

All of these are foods that need to be consumed in moderation. Recognize that they are often hidden ingredients within other foods. Therefore, it is wise to limit your intake wherever possible to make sure you aren't putting too much of these items into your body.

Part of your physical health is also caring for your brain. Think of it as a muscle. Like every muscle in your body, it is important to allow it to relax and get the necessary rest. This can be done through meditation or even finding some quiet time away from your family and friends to relax and think quietly without distraction. Doing so also allows you to reduce your stress level. Making sure your stress level comes down will positively impact your mental health as well.

Do you have a place that brings you peace? Having this place allows you to mentally unwind and just let go of your stress, even if it is just temporarily. Meditation is a method that you can use, even if all you can do is go to a quiet place in your home or office. There are a variety of meditation techniques available. Some individuals prefer a calming form of music to accompany their meditation, while others prefer to just enjoy the silence. Whatever you prefer, the point is to make your mental health a priority. If you do, it will be much easier to handle change and thrive.

Change can bring benefits and give us opportunities we might not otherwise have considered without the upheaval in our lives. But in order to benefit from change, we need to maintain our positivity, both physically and mentally. This can be hard to do when a change has a particularly emotional impact. Relying on family and friends for support is key to dealing with the more emotional aspects of any change in your life.

Throughout this discussion of your health, I haven't really touched on one area that impacts our well-being. That is our relationships. But how do they impact our lives and what do we need to remember about these relationships when it comes to change?

KEY #4. RELATIONSHIPS

Did you know that you are shaped by the people you spend the most time with? Those individuals will influence your ideas, beliefs, and actions. This also extends to your attitude. If you are surrounded by positive thinkers, it is much easier to maintain a positive attitude. Think about the last time you were surrounded by negative individuals. After a while, did it seem as if that negative and critical spirit rubbed off on you?

Here are some questions to ask yourself about the people you spend time with. Are they primarily positive or negative? Do you find yourself having spirited conversations with plenty of give and take, or do you find that you are just a dumping ground for all their complaints about life?

If you want to create change in your life or be more accepting of the changes in your life, then you may need to assess who you spend most of your time with. Creating a new attitude or shifting your thought process means assessing who is influencing them both and whether that influence is helping or hurting.

When I was finishing my university education, I was associating with a group of friends who were eager to join the corporate world. I had worked in the corporate world during my summer breaks, but I had also started a business installing sprinkler systems in areas where there was new home construction. I did this after hours and on weekends. Although I was working a lot, I was also figuring out that I didn't have to go the corporate route to be successful. My small part-time business had made me more money than my daily corporate job.

Our final year of school came and, of course, my friends and I discussed what our next steps were as we started life after university. Some had mixed feelings about what direction to take after graduating. The options included attempting to open a business in the role of entrepreneur or applying to one of the many companies out there for a traditional corporate role.

Since most of my friends decided to go the corporate route, I did too, even though my experience indicated that I could be equally, if not more, successful in the role of entrepreneur. The individuals I associated with provided acknowledgement and support during that decision-making period of my life.

Are there some decisions where you can see the influence of your associates? Can you look back now and see that perhaps a different decision would have been more appropriate for the path you ultimately wanted to pursue?

While we all want to think that we are independent thinkers, sudden influences from our associates can impact what we choose to do and how we think and act. Yet, with a greater understanding of who you are as a person (your goals and your passions), you will find that you can truly be an independent thinker and identify the effect of those influences around you.

Self-knowledge takes time, but the reward is a better way to embrace life and the change around us, both personally and professionally. If you want to move down a specific path toward your goal, you need to make sure to associate with like-minded individuals. They can encourage and support you as you work to achieve those specific milestones.

As you discover what you are passionate about, you will be able to find like-minded friends and associates who are focused on that particular activity or pursuit. For instance, you may be passionate about helping young people. There may be local groups geared toward providing activities and mentorship to teenagers within your community. Getting involved in those groups will put you around others who share your passion, which can help motivate you even further.

Take the time to examine your beliefs and determine if the friends you are associating with are the right people to support you in the next stage or season of your life. Not everyone you spend time with will be an active part of helping you achieve your goals. However, they can be the individuals who make you laugh, as well as help you see the positive when situations or circumstances seem overwhelming.

The point is to be around people who embrace change and can help you to do the same. When it comes to your mindset, negative association will eventually bring even the most positive mindset down. Have you ever tried to accomplish something that you had already decided was impossible? It becomes an uphill battle, and you likely didn't succeed.

A positive attitude, on the other hand, makes it possible for you to achieve even more than you thought was possible. In addition, your positive mindset could have an influence on those around you. Imagine being a positive influence to those who are important to you. The best relationships are the ones where you both are actively working to support and encourage each other in pursuit of your passions, while being there for each other during times of major change or upheaval that life seems to throw at us all.

If you are looking to make adjustments to your circle of friends and associates, consider looking into your community for opportunities to meet new people. Some ideas include joining a club or charity organization. If there is an activity that you have been interested in trying, why not sign up for lessons? What things have you been afraid to try for one reason or another? Why not give one of those things a try? If your fear is that you won't do well, make peace with that and do it anyway. You might find that as you conquer your fear, you make new friends that will enrich your life.

I want to point out here that the idea is to make you better able to adapt to change and train yourself to see the benefit of change versus focusing on the fear and anxiety. Each of these new experiences is putting you in charge of creating change in your life on a smaller scale, which will make it easier for you to handle change on a larger scale.

The most rewarding sport even for me was signing up and participating in triathlons. I was a prairie boy who didn't grow up around water. Signing up for a triathlon forced me to learn how to swim. I could have let fear of the unknown stop me, but instead I broadened my horizons.

Additionally, I signed up with a friend. We challenged each other and held each other accountable for attaining our goals. It was not an easy journey, but I found new strength as I pushed myself and supported my friend.

The 10-month journey before my first triathlon was grueling at times. It included swim lessons, getting the proper equipment, the proper bike, the right shoes, and more. After those 10 months of training, lessons, and standing up to my own fears, the day of the race finally came.

The first leg of the triathlon was swimming, which I can definitely say was not my strength. In fact, when I ran into the water, I was with a pack of men, but after a few minutes of kicking and banging around, I was alone and about ready to give up. Instead of doing that, I pulled back for a moment, composed myself, and then started to swim, concentrating on one stroke at a time.

I finished dead last in the swim, but at least I finished. I continued with ease to do the bike and run, completing those two legs in top times. I was dead last overall, because of my slow swim, but I still felt a great sense of accomplishment because I had completed my goal. In the process, I had met many new people who shared an interest in triathlons. I also got closer to my friend Nick, who trained with me and completed the same triathlon.

It was a rewarding event for me, not only because I actually finished what I set out to do, but because when I went out to celebrate that night, I met my future wife. Our relationship has been full of change and challenges, but none of the joys would have been possible if I hadn't stepped outside of my comfort zone to try something new and conquered a fear at the same time.

Think about the various relationships in your life. Could there be someone who is already in your life who would be supportive as you step outside your comfort zone? Those individuals are the ones who will support you through change. They are key relationships to nurture. Still, those relationships will not be able to support you if you are not able to communicate your needs to those critical people in your life. As a result, my fifth key is also the most critical: communication.

KEY #5. COMMUNICATION

No matter who we are and what we do throughout the day, we are constantly communicating. We use our faces, our hands, and, of course, our speech to communicate what we are thinking and feeling on a daily basis.

Yet within the realm of communication, the opportunities for misunderstandings abound. There are literally hundreds of thousands of examples throughout history demonstrating how misunderstandings can grow into much larger breakdowns of relationships between individuals, groups, and even countries.

Communication is truly an incredible concept. Great communicators can wow us and bring difficult concepts or ideas into focus. Have you ever heard the speeches of Martin Luther King Jr.? Decades after his passing, his words continue to move people. Then there are more current examples, such as Tony Robbins, Bob Proctor, or Brian Tracy. All of these individuals are amazing in their delivery of self-help information. Listen to their presentations and you can see how they really connect with their audiences.

Change requires communication, but change doesn't go over well if it is not communicated well. Every parent who communicates with a teenager can appreciate this point. Their child may not be able to articulate their frustration or the reasons behind it. An argument often becomes par for the course, leaving everyone frustrated and out of sorts. Misunderstandings can make change difficult to handle, because you may not understand why the change is occurring.

Companies often make this mistake as well. They may not clearly communicate their vision, so when they make changes, their employees are often left feeling frustrated and out of the loop. It can also make them feel uncertain about their job security, which can negatively impact their productivity. The reality is that miscommunication can have a large impact on whether change is welcomed or feared.

Communication is more than just speaking clearly. It is listening to and understanding the concerns of the other person and doing your best to address those concerns. When it comes to creating change in your life, you may find that you need to explain to your family why you are making that change. How do you communicate your choice? Often, how well it is communicated is reflected in the level of support you receive and if the change is embraced or not.

Have you been part of a change where the communication was less than you expected? How did that impact your ability to accept the change and create something incredible from that opportunity? For many of us, the answer is that the change was more difficult and we likely didn't support it wholeheartedly.

Again, the point is that communication can make a change easier to accept or a lack of it can make the implementation of a change more difficult. If you are initiating change in your own life, be sure that you are clearly communicating your needs to those around you. While they may not always agree with your decisions, they are much more likely to support them and the changes you want to make if you can clearly communicate the change and its impact.

Along with good communication, you need to be a good listener. Often misunderstandings occur because one individual is not really listening to the other. They may miss key instructions or details that could make the situation clearer. As a result, it can be easy to act without truly knowing all the necessary facts and circumstances. Can you see how not listening well could impact how you feel about a change in your life? It is also easy to see how others might be less supportive of change you initiate if they weren't listening.

How can you tell if someone is truly hearing you? Ask them questions and then clarify when it appears that they may not have gotten an accurate picture of what is about to occur. Some individuals may want to willfully misunderstand, and you want to do everything in your power to avoid that. At the same time, be a good listener. Don't listen to respond, but listen to understand their concerns, worries, and potential fears. Make adjustments to address their concerns where possible, but be as reassuring as you can when those adjustments might not be possible.

When you don't listen, you run the risk of missing key instructions or information that could directly impact your life or the change you are about to make.

I was always working, even from a young age. For a period of time, I worked on a gravel crusher as a ground person. My job was to go around and check for broken wheels, conveyors, and signs of wear and tear on other components. If something was wrong, I was to report it immediately to the tower person overseeing the operation. His job was to shut down the entire mechanical operation so the problem could be addressed. If he didn't, a major failure could occur, which could end up costing thousands of dollars of damage.

One morning, I was tired and didn't pay attention when I was relieving the previous shift. I had missed that a flashing was tearing and did not report it. An hour later, that flashing tore through. My boss saw it first. Gravel was everywhere. He had the operation stopped, then came over to the tool shack to fire me for not properly checking the system. That miscommunication cost the company time and money, plus I lost my job. The lesson? Communication and paying attention to the details is key to success in any area of your life, but especially when you are initiating major change.

Now let's talk about how a lack of communication can contribute to conflict. Our ability to connect with others can be hampered if we don't communicate well or if we are not sensitive to their needs and hot spots. Our personal and professional lives can be impacted by poor communication.

If you are considering acting to make changes in your life, start with how you communicate with others. We can all find areas to improve and make our connections with others deeper and more meaningful. The art of language is not easy. From birth, we are trained to communicate, but it doesn't come easily to all of us. Some become better than others at expressing themselves. The art of communication can be terrifying and amazing at the same time. You may also find it difficult to express yourself, especially when dealing with loved ones. How can you communicate more effectively with the individuals in your life?

Start by asking questions. This helps you gather information. Repeat back to the speaker your understanding of what they just said in response to your question. If they don't agree with your interpretation, keep asking for clarification until you get it. Be sure that you genuinely listen to the response before you start making assumptions. Try and imagine the situation from the other person's point of view. Be patient, because the best communication takes time.

There are also classes on public speaking and the art of communication. If you find yourself struggling consistently in this area, consider taking a course. The principles and real-world practice can help you improve your general communication skills. If you find yourself losing your train of thought, then consider writing down what you want to say. Be clear and concise where possible. Then use your written thoughts as a platform to bring up various points when appropriate within the context of the conversation.

Don't underestimate the power of practicing your communication skills in front of a mirror. This is where you can work on eye contact, exploring your various facial expressions, and also how to speak clearly. If you can talk to yourself, then it will get easier to talk to others. Make an effort to come out of your comfort zone, especially if you are not a good communicator. Consider it a change for the better.

Recognize that by improving your communication skills you can improve the quality of your life, as well as weather changing circumstances more effectively.

MOVE FORWARD WITH ME

Throughout this chapter, I have focused on some key areas that can make change more palatable, and reduce the fear and anxiety that commonly occurs. Still, the reality is that change, especially change we didn't initiate, can be overwhelming. Over the course of my lifetime, I have dealt with a variety of changes and I can say that not every experience was pleasant. But they all taught me valuable lessons.

I also want to remind you that change doesn't need to be something that occurs to you, but can be something you initiate. Consider areas of your life that are not as satisfying as you would like them to be. For example, are you struggling financially, but find yourself reluctant to make changes or take the risks necessary to turn your financial life around? Here is an area where making a change happen can have a significant impact.

However, don't limit yourself merely to material affluence. There are literally dozens of areas where you could find yourself hesitating to make changes. No matter what change you want to make, the mindset you choose will determine whether the change is successful or a struggle.

Throughout my work with individuals on changes in their lives, one thing has become clear; your mindset is key to making change work for you and allowing yourself to embrace change effectively.

I'm willing to work with you to help create the change that you want to see in your life. Let's face it, changes to our self-belief can lead to even more significant changes in other areas of our lives. With an improvement to your self-belief, there is no telling what you can accomplish. The changes to your point of view about yourself and what you can accomplish will help you make different choices about how you choose to live and work.

I believe that coaching is key to creating the right mindset to initiate and absorb changes in your life. A positive mindset allows you to see change in terms of what is possible, instead of focusing on the potential losses. Until you take the leap, you will never know exactly what is possible. But it can be hard to take those first steps to overhauling your thought process on your own.

I believe strongly in coaching and mentorship. It is a way to pass on the wisdom you have learned and the key strategies you may have discovered for addressing and initiating change. As part of my efforts to help others embrace change, my coaching and mentorship is available to you.

In my book, The Book of Change, I tackle a variety of topics and areas where you can start making small changes to build up to bigger ones. I also discuss how you can take dramatic and difficult circumstances and use them to learn and grow.

Using these tools, you can make a difference in your own life and in the lives of others. You can go from being fearful of change to being an example of embracing change for those in your family, your social circle, and your community. However, coaching isn't the only way to work on your skills to create and embrace change.

You can become a change advocate. That means allowing your positive mindset regarding change to influence others and impact their attitudes toward possible changes in their own lives. Your own example of dealing with change can serve as inspiration for others, which can then allow them to turn themselves into change advocates. It is a never ending cycle, which can give you peace of mind, even when faced with the toughest of challenges.

Additionally, there are other key takeaways for you to keep in mind as you start the journey to create change in your life. One way to embrace it is to understand what is happening and even to learn why.

Continuing education allows you to take the fear out of any change. After all, most of the fear of change stems from a lack of knowledge about what the change will mean for you, your family, and your community. When we are informed, change can be less intimidating, which can make us less fearful and more willing to take risks. Change is a part of taking risks to grow and explore our passions, achieve our goals, and fulfill our dreams. Without the right information and mindset, we will be unwilling to take the risks needed to achieve everything we imagine possible.

Clearly, you need to remember that change is a constant in your life. No one can escape it, no matter how risk adverse they may be. You need to embrace change for the benefits it can provide by creating a different mindset, gaining new skills, or even just acknowledging the personal growth that has resulted.

The change you see in your lifetime can and likely will have a profound impact on the lives of others, both now and in the future. Respect the people around you and demonstrate love and support when they are faced with changes, both large and small.

Contact me at **tony@tonydebogorski.com**. I would love to explore the ways that I can help you create real change in your life through adjustments to your mindset and increasing your willingness to learn and explore. Be inspired to create the meaningful life that you have always wanted and step away from living in fear of the unknown.

Amazing things are waiting for you! It is time for you to take the first step towards being a change agent in your own life.

Branding Small Business

RAYMOND AARON

B randing is an incredibly important tool for creating and building your business. Large companies have been benefiting from branding ever since people first started selling things to other people. Branding made those businesses big.

If you're a small business owner, you probably imagine that small companies are different and don't need branding as much as large companies do. Not true. The truth is small businesses need branding just as much, if not more, than large companies.

Perhaps you've thought about branding, but assumed you'd need millions of dollars to do it properly, or that branding is just the same thing as marketing. Nothing could be further from the truth.

Marketing is the engine of your company's success. Branding is the fuel in that engine.

In the old days, salespeople were a big part of the selling process. They recommended one product over another and laid out the reasons why it was better. Salespeople had credibility because they knew about all the products, and customers often took the advice they had to offer.

Today, consumers control the buying process. They shop in big box stores, super-sized supermarkets, and over the Internet — where there are no salespeople. Buyers now get online and gather information beforehand. They learn about all the products available and look to see if there really is any difference between them. Consumers also read reviews and check social media to see if both the company and the product are reputable. In other words, they want to know what the brand is all about.

The way of commerce used to be: "Nothing happens till something is sold." Today it's: "Nothing happens till something is branded!"

DEFINING A BRAND

A brand is a proper name that stands for something. It lives in the consumer's mind, has positive or negative characteristics, and invokes a feeling or an image. In short, it's a person's perception of a product or a company.

When all goes well, consumers associate the same characteristics with a brand that the company talks about in its advertising, public relations, marketing and sales materials. Of course, when a product doesn't live up to what the company says about it, the brand gets a bad reputation. On the other hand, if a product or service over-delivers on the promises made, the brand can become a superstar.

RECOGNIZING BRANDING AND ITS CHARACTERISTICS

Branding is the science and art of making something that isn't unique, unique. Branding in the marketplace is the same as branding on a ranch. On a ranch, ranchers use branding to differentiate their cattle from every other rancher's cattle (because all cattle look pretty much the same). In the marketplace, branding is what makes a product stand out in a crowd of similar products. The right branding gets you noticed, remembered and sold — or perhaps I should say bought, because today it is all about buying, not selling.

There are four main characteristics of branding that make it an integral part of the marketing and purchasing process.

1. Branding makes you trustworthy and known

Branding makes a product more special than other products. With branding, a normal, everyday product has a personality, and a first and last name, and people know who you are.

In today's marketplace, most products are, more or less, just like their competition. Toilet paper is toilet paper, milk is milk, and a grocery store by any other name is still a grocery store. However, branding takes a product and makes it unique. For example, high-quality drinking water is available from just about every tap in the Western world and it's free, but people pay good money for it when it comes in a bottle. Branding takes bottled water and makes Evian.

Furthermore, every aspect of your brand gives potential customers a feeling or comfort level that they associate with you. The more powerful and positive that feeling is, the more easily and more frequently they will want to do business with you and, indeed, will do business with you.

2. Branding differentiates you from others

Strong branding makes you better than your competition, and makes your product name memorable and easy to remember. Even if your product is absolutely the same as every other product like it, branding makes it special. Branding makes it the first product a consumer thinks about when deciding to make a purchase.

Branding also makes a product seem popular. Everyone knows about it, which implicitly says people like it. And, if people like it, it must be good.

3. Branding makes you worth more money

The stronger your branding is, the more likely people are willing to spend that little bit extra because they believe you, your product, your service, or your business are worth it. They may say they won't, but they will. They do it all the time.

For example, a one-pound box of Godiva chocolates costs about $40; the same weight of Hershey's Kisses costs about $4. The quality of the chocolate isn't ten times greater. The reason people buy Godiva is that the brand Godiva means "gift" whereas the brand Hershey means "snack". Gifts obviously cost more than snacks.

4. Branding pre-sells your product

In the buying age, people most often make the decision on which products to pick up before they walk into the store. The stronger the branding, the more likely people are to think in terms of your product rather than the product category. For example, people are as likely, maybe even more likely, to add Hellmann's to the shopping list as they are to write down simply mayo. The same is true for soda, ketchup, and many other products with successful, strong branding.

Plus, as soon as a shopper gets to the shelf, branding can provide a quick reminder of what products to grab in a few ways:

- An icon or logo
- A specific color
- An audio icon

BRANDING IN A SMALL BUSINESS

Big companies spend millions of dollars on advertising, marketing, and public relations (PR) to build recognition of a new product name. They get their selling messages out to the public using television, radio, magazines, and the Internet. They can even throw money at damage control when necessary. The strategies for branding are the same in a small business, but the scale, costs, and a few of the tactics change.

Make your brand name work harder

The name of a small business can mean everything in terms of branding. Your brand name needs to work harder for your business than you do. It's the first thing a prospective customer sees, and it is how they will remember you. A brand name has to be memorable when spoken, and focused in its meaning. If the name doesn't represent what consumers believe about a product and the company that makes it, then that brand will fail.

In building your product's reputation and image, less is often significantly more. Make sure the name you choose immediately gives a sense of what you do.

Large corporations have millions of dollars to take a meaningless brand name and make it stand for something. Small businesses don't, so use words that really mean something. Strive for something interesting and be right on point. You don't need to be boring.

Plumbers, for example, would do well setting themselves apart with names like "The On-Time Plumber" or "24/7 Plumbing". The same is true for electricians, IT providers, or even marketing consultants. Plenty of other types of business are so general in nature they just don't work hard enough in a business or product name.

Even the playing field: The Net

The Internet has leveled the playing field for small businesses like nothing else. You can use the Internet in several ways to market your brand:

Website: Developing and maintaining a website is easier than ever. Anyone can find your business regardless of its size.

Social Media: Facebook and Twitter can promote your brand in a cost-effective manner.

BUILDING YOUR BRAND WITH THE BRANDING LADDER

Even if you do everything perfectly the first time (and I don't know anyone who does), branding takes time. How much time isn't just up to you, but you can speed things along by understanding the different levels of branding, as well as the business and marketing strategies that can get you to the top.

Introducing the Branding Ladder

Moving through the levels of branding is like climbing a ladder to the top of the marketplace. The Branding Ladder has five distinct rungs and, unlike stairs, you can't take them two at a time. You have to take them in order, and some businesses spend more time on each rung than others.

You can also think of the Branding Ladder in terms of a scale from zero to ten. Everyone starts at zero. If you properly climb the ladder, you can end up at 12 out of 10. The Branding Ladder below shows a special rung at the top of the ladder that can take your business over the top. The following section explains the Branding Ladder and how your small business can move up it.

THE BRANDING LADDER	
Brand Advocacy	12/10
Brand Insistence	10/10
Brand Preference	3/10
Brand Awareness	1/10
Brand Absence	0/10

Rung 1: Living in the void

Your business, in fact every business, starts at the bottom rung, which is called brand absence, meaning you have no brand whatsoever except your own name. On a scale of one to ten, brand absence is, of course, zero. That's the worst place to live and obviously the most difficult entrepreneurially. The good news is that the only way is up.

Ninety-seven percent of businesses live on this rung of the Branding Ladder. They earn far less than they want to earn, far less than they should earn, and far less than they would earn if they did exactly the same work under a real brand.

Rung 2: Achieving awareness

Brand awareness is a good first step up the ladder to the second rung. Actually, it's really good, especially because 97 percent of businesses never get there. You want people to be aware of you. When person A speaks to person B and says, "Have you heard of "The 24/7 Plumber?" You want the answer to be "yes".

On that scale of one to ten, however, brand awareness is only a one. It's better than nothing, but not that much better. Although people know of your brand, being aware doesn't mean that they are interested in buying it. Coca Cola drinkers know about Pepsi, but they don't drink it.

Rung 3: Becoming the preferred brand

Getting to the third rung, brand preference, is definitely a real step up. This rung means that people prefer to use your product or service rather than that of your competition. They believe there is a real difference between you and others, and you're their first choice. This rung is a crucial branding stage for parity products, such as bottled water and breakfast cereals, not to mention plumbers, electricians, lawyers, and all the others. Brand preference is clearly better than brand awareness, but it's less than halfway up the ladder.

Car rental companies represent a perfect example of why brand preference may not be enough. When someone lands at an airport and needs to rent a car on the spot, he or she may go straight to the preferred rental counter. If that company has a car available, it's a sale. However, if all the cars for that company have been rented, the person will move to the next rental kiosk without much thought, because one rental car is just as good as another.

Exerting Brand Preference needs to be easy and convenient

If all you have is brand preference, your business is on shaky ground and you can lose business for the feeblest of reasons. Very few people go to a second or third supermarket just to find their favorite brand of bottled water. Similarly, a shopper may prefer one store over another but, if both stores sell the same products, he or she will often go to the closest store even if it is not the better liked one. The reason for staying nearby does not need to be a dramatic one — the shopper may simply be tired, on a tight schedule, or not in the mood to travel.

Rung 4: Making it you and only you

When your customers are so committed to your product or service that they won't accept a substitute, you have reached the fourth rung of the Branding Ladder. All companies strive to reach this place, called brand insistence.

Brand insistence means that someone's experience with a product in terms of performance, durability, customer service, and image has been sufficiently exceptional. As a result, the product has earned an incredible level of loyalty. If the product isn't available where the customer is, he or she will literally not buy something else. Rather, the person will look for the preferred product elsewhere. Can you imagine what a fabulous place this is for a company to be? Brand insistence is the best of the best, the perfect ten out of ten, the whole ball of wax.

Apple is a perfect example of brand insistence

Apple users don't just think, they know in their heads and hearts, that anything made by Apple is technologically-advanced, user-friendly, and just all-around superior. Committed to everything Apple, Mac users won't even entertain the thought that a PC may have positive attributes.

Apple people love everything about their Macs, iPads, iPhones, the Mac stores and all those apps. When the company introduces a new product, many of its brand-insistent fans actually wait in line overnight to be one of the first to have it. Steve Jobs is one of their idols.

Considering one big potential problem

Unfortunately, you can lose brand insistence much more quickly than you can achieve it. Brand-insistent customers have such high expectations that they can be disillusioned or disappointed by just one bad product experience. You also have to consistently reinforce the positives because insistence can fade over time. Even someone who has bought and re-bought a specific brand of car for the last 20 years can decide it's just time for a change. That's how fickle the world is.

At ten out of ten, brand insistence may seem like the top rung of the ladder, but it's not. One rung is actually better, and it involves getting your brand-insistent customers to keep polishing your brand for you.

Rung 5: Getting customers to do the work for you

Brand advocacy is the highest rung on the ladder. It's better than ten out of ten because you have customers who are so happy with your product that they want everyone to know about it and use it. Think of them as uber-fans. Not only do they recommend you to friends and family, they also practically shout your praises from the rooftops, interrupt conversations among strangers to give their opinion, and tell everyone they meet how fantastic you are. Most companies can only aspire to this level of customer satisfaction. Apple is one of the few large corporations in recent history that has brand advocates all over the world.

- Brand advocacy does the following five extraordinary things for your company. Brand advocacy:

- Provides a level of visibility that you couldn't pay for if you tried. Brand advocates are so enthusiastic they talk about you all the time, and reach people in ways general media and public relations can't. You get great visibility because they make sure people actually listen.

- Delivers free advertising and public relations. Companies love the extra super-positive messaging, all for free.

- Affords a level of credibility that literally can't be bought. Brand advocates are more than just walking testimonials. They are living proof that you are the best.

- Provides pre-sold prospective customers. Advocate recommendations carry so much weight that they are worth much more than plain referrals. They deliver customers ready and committed to purchasing your product or service.

- Increases profits exponentially. Brand advocates are money-making machines for your business because they increase sales and decrease marketing costs.

For these reasons, brand advocacy is 12 out of 10!!

BRANDING YOURSELF: HOW TO DO SO IN FOUR EASY WAYS

If you're interested in branding your product or company, you may not be sure where to begin. The good news: I'm here to help. You can brand in many ways, but here I pare it down to four ways to help you start:

Branding by association

This way involves hanging out with and being seen with people who are very much higher than you in your particular niche.

Branding by achievement

This way repurposes your previous achievements.

Branding by testimonial

This way makes use of the testimonials that you receive but have likely never used.

Branding by WOW

A WOW is the pleasantly unexpected, the equivalent of going the extra mile. The easiest and most certain way to WOW people is to tell them that you've written a book. To discover how you can write a book on your own, please go to www.BrandingSmallBusinessForDummies.com.

Happiness: How to Experience the "Real Deals"

MARCI SHIMOFF

I was 41 years old, stretched out on a lounge chair by my pool and reflecting on my life. I had achieved all that I thought I needed to be happy.

You see, when I was a child, I thought there would be five main things that would ensure that I'd be happy: a successful career helping people, a loving husband, a comfortable home, a great body, and a wonderful circle of friends. After years of study, hard work, and a few "lucky breaks," I finally had them all. (Okay, so my body didn't quite look like Halle Berry's—but four out of five isn't bad!) You think I'd have been on the top of the world.

But surprisingly I wasn't. I felt an emptiness inside that the outer successes of life couldn't fill. I was also afraid that if I lost any of those things, I might be miserable. Sadly, I knew I wasn't alone in feeling this way.

While happiness is the one thing we all truly want, so few people really experience the deep and lasting fulfillment that fills our soul. Why aren't we finding it?

Because, in the words of the old country western song, we're looking for happiness in "all the wrong places."

Looking around, I saw that the happiest people I knew weren't the most successful and famous. Some were married, some were single. Some had lots of money, and some didn't have a dime. Some of them even had health challenges. From where I stood, there seemed to be no rhyme or reason to what made people happy. The obvious question became: *Could a person actually be happy for no reason?*

I had to find out.

So I threw myself into the study of happiness. I interviewed scores of scientists, as well as 100 unconditionally happy people. (I call them the Happy 100.) I delved into the research from the burgeoning field of positive psychology, the study of the positive traits that enable people to enjoy meaningful, fulfilling, and happy lives.

What I found changed my life. To share this knowledge with others, I wrote a book called *Happy for No Reason: 7 Steps to Being Happy from the Inside Out.*

One day, as I sat down to compile my findings, all the pieces of the puzzle fell into place. I had a simple, but profound "a-ha"—there's a continuum of happiness:

Unhappy	Happy for Bad Reason	Happy for Good Reason	Happy for No Reason
Depressed	High from unhealthy addictions	Satisfaction from healthy experiences	Inner state of peace & well-being

EXTERNAL — INTERNAL

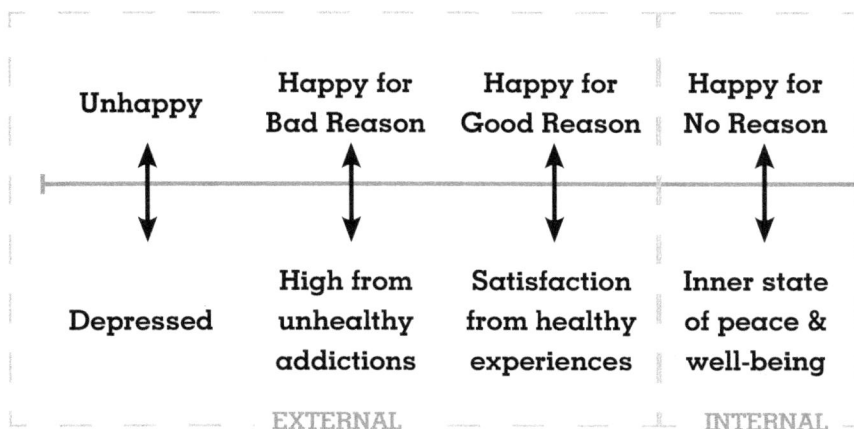

Unhappy: We all know what this means: life seems flat. Some of the signs are anxiety, fatigue, feeling blue or low—your "garden-variety" unhappiness. This isn't the same as clinical depression, which is characterized by deep despair and hopelessness that dramatically interferes with your ability to live a normal life, and for which professional help is absolutely necessary.

Happy for Bad Reason: When people are unhappy, they often try to make themselves feel better by indulging in addictions or behaviors that may feel good in the moment but are ultimately detrimental. They seek the highs that come from drugs, alcohol, excessive sex, "retail therapy," compulsive gambling, over-eating, and too much television-watching, to name a few. This kind of "happiness" is hardly happiness at all. It is only a temporary way to numb or escape our unhappiness through fleeting experiences of pleasure.

Happy for Good Reason: This is what people usually mean by happiness: having good relationships with our family and friends, success in our careers, financial security, a nice house or car, or using our talents and strengths well. It's the pleasure we derive from having the healthy things in our lives that we want.

Don't get me wrong. I'm all for this kind of happiness! It's just that it's only half the story. Being Happy for Good Reason depends on the external conditions of our lives—these conditions change or are lost, our happiness usually goes too. Relying solely on this type of happiness is where a lot of our fear is stemming from these days. We're afraid the things we think we need to be happy may be slipping from our grasp.

Deep inside, I think we all know that life isn't meant to be about getting by, numbing our pain, or having everything "under control." True happiness doesn't come from merely collecting an assortment of happy experiences. At our core, we know there's something more than this.

There is. It's the next level on the happiness continuum—Happy for No Reason.

Happy for No Reason: This is true happiness—a state of peace and well-being that isn't dependent on external circumstances.

Happy for No Reason isn't elation, euphoria, mood spikes, or peak experiences that don't last. It doesn't mean grinning like a fool 24/7 or experiencing a superficial high. Happy for No Reason isn't an emotion. In fact, when you are Happy for No Reason, you can have *any* emotion—including sadness, fear, anger or hurt—but you still experience that underlying state of peace and well-being.

When you're Happy for No Reason, you *bring* happiness to your outer experiences rather than trying to *extract* happiness from them. You don't need to manipulate the world around you to try to make yourself happy. You live from happiness, rather than *for* happiness.

This is a revolutionary concept. Most of us focus on being Happy for Good Reason, stringing together as many happy experiences as we can, like beads in a necklace, to create a happy life. We have to spend a lot of time and energy trying to find just the right beads so we can have a "happy necklace".

Being Happy for No Reason, in our necklace analogy, is like having a happy string. No matter what beads we put on our necklace—good, bad or indifferent—our inner experience, which is the string that runs through them all, is happy, and creates a happy life.

Happy for No Reason is a state that's been spoken of in virtually all spiritual and religious traditions throughout history. The concept is universal. In Buddhism, it is called causeless joy; in Christianity, the kingdom of Heaven within; and in Judaism it is called *ashrei*, an inner sense of holiness and health. In Islam it is called *falah*, happiness and well-being; and in Hinduism it is called *ananda*, or pure bliss. Some traditions refer to it as an enlightened or awakened state.

So how can you be Happy for No Reason?

Science is verifying the way. Researchers in the field of positive psychology have found that we each have a "happiness set-point," that determines our level of happiness. No matter what happens, whether it's something as exhilarating as winning the lottery or as challenging as a horrible accident, most people eventually return to their original happiness level. Like your weight set-point, which keeps the scale hovering around the same number, your happiness set-point will remain the same **unless you make a concerted effort to change it.** In the same way you'd crank up the thermostat to get comfortable on a chilly day, you actually have the power to reprogram your happiness set-point to a higher level of peace and well-being. The secret lies in practicing the habits of happiness.

Some books and programs will tell you that you can simply decide to be happy. They say just make up your mind to be happy—and you will be.

I don't agree.

You can't just decide to be happy, any more than you can decide to be fit or to be a great piano virtuoso and expect instant mastery. You can, however, decide to take the necessary steps, like exercising or taking piano lessons—and by practicing those skills, you can get in shape or give recitals. In the same way, you can become Happy for No Reason through practicing the habits of happy people.

All of your habitual thoughts and behaviors in the past have created specific neural pathways in the wiring in your brain, like grooves in a record. When we think or behave a certain way over and over, the neural pathway is strengthened and the groove becomes deeper—the way a well-traveled route through a field eventually becomes a clear-cut path. Unhappy people tend to have more negative neural pathways. This is why you can't just ignore the realities of your brain's wiring and *decide* to be happy! To raise your level of happiness, you have to create new grooves.

Scientists used to think that once a person reached adulthood, the brain was fairly well "set in stone" and there wasn't much you could do to change it. But new research is revealing exciting information about the brain's neuroplasticity: when you think, feel and act in different ways, the brain changes and actually rewires itself. You aren't doomed to the same negative neural pathways for your whole life. Leading brain researcher Dr. Richard Davidson, of the University of Wisconsin says, "Based on what we know of the plasticity of the brain, we can think of things like happiness and compassion as skills that are no different from learning to play a musical instrument or tennis …. it is possible to train our brains to be happy."

While a few of the Happy 100 I interviewed were born happy, most of them learned to be happy by practicing habits that supported their happiness. That means wherever you are on the happiness continuum, it's entirely in your power to raise your happiness level.

In the course of my research, I uncovered 21 core happiness habits that anyone can use to become happier and stay that way. You can find all 21 happiness habits at www.HappyForNoReason.com

Here are a few tips to get you started:

1. **Incline Your Mind Toward Joy.** Have you noticed that your mind tends to register the negative events in your life more than the positive? If you get ten compliments in a day and one criticism, what do you remember? For most people, it's the criticism. Scientists call this our "negativity bias" — our primitive survival wiring that causes us to pay more attention to the negative than the positive. To reverse this bias, get into the daily habit of consciously registering the positive around you: the sun on your skin, the taste of a favorite food, a smile or kind word from a co-worker or friend. Once you notice something positive, take a moment to savor it deeply and feel it; make it more than just a mental observation. Spend 20 seconds soaking up the happiness you feel.

2. **Let Love Lead.** One way to power up your heart's flow is by sending loving kindness to your friends and family, as well as strangers you pass on the street. Next time you're waiting for the elevator at work, stuck in a line at the store or caught up in traffic, send a silent wish to the people you see for their happiness, well-being, and health. Simply wishing others well switches on the "pump" in your own heart that generates love and creates a strong current of happiness.

3. **Lighten Your Load.** To make a habit of letting go of worries and negative thoughts, start by letting go on the physical level. Cultural anthropologist Angeles Arrien recommends giving or throwing away 27 items a day for nine days. This deceptively simple practice will help you break attachments that no longer serve you.

4. **Make Your Cells Happy.** Your brain contains a veritable pharmacopeia of natural happiness-enhancing neurochemicals — endorphins, serotonin, oxytocin, and dopamine — just waiting to be released to every organ and cell in your body. The way that you eat, move, rest, and even your facial expression can shift the balance of your body's feel-good-chemicals, or "Joy Juice", in your favor. To dispense some extra Joy Juice — smile. Scientists have discovered that smiling decreases stress hormones and boosts happiness chemicals, which increase the body's T-cells, reduce pain, and enhance relaxation. You may not feel like it, but smiling — even artificially to begin with — starts the ball rolling and will turn into a real smile in short order.

5. **Hang with the Happy.** We catch the emotions of those around us just like we catch their colds — it's called emotional contagion. So it's important to make wise choices about the company you keep. Create appropriate boundaries with emotional bullies and "happiness vampires" who suck the life out of you. Develop your happiness "dream team" — a mastermind or support group you meet with regularly to keep you steady on the path of raising your happiness.

"Happily ever after" isn't just for fairytales or for only the lucky few. Imagine experiencing inner peace and well-being as the backdrop for everything else in your life. When you're Happy for No Reason, it's not that your life always looks perfect — it's that, however it looks, you'll still be happy!

By Marci Shimoff. Based on the New York Times bestseller *Happy for No Reason: 7 Steps to Being Happy from the Inside Out*, which offers a revolutionary approach to experiencing deep and lasting happiness. The woman's face of the *Chicken Soup for the Soul* series and a featured teacher in *The Secret*, Marci is an authority on success, happiness, and the law of attraction. To order *Happy for No Reason* and receive free bonus gifts, go to www.happyfornoreason.com/mybook.

Sex, Love and Relationships

DR. JOHN GRAY

Just as great sex is important to lasting love, good health is important to sex and relationships. About 12 years ago, I cured myself of early stage Parkinson's disease. The doctors were amazed, but my wife was even more amazed. She noted that our relationship and sex life had become dramatically better. It turns out that the natural supplements I used to reverse Parkinson's can also make you more attentive and loving in your relationship. At that point, I realized that good relationship skills alone were not enough to sustain love and passion for a lifetime.

I shared many insights gained from my 40 years' experience as a marriage counselor and coach in *Men Are From Mars, Women Are From Venus*. And while my insights go a long way towards helping men and women understand and support each other, good communication skills alone are not always enough. For better relationships, we not only need to be healthy, but we must also experience optimum brain function.

If you are tired, depressed, anxious, not sleeping well, or in pain, then certainly romantic feelings will become a thing of the past. My recovery from Parkinson's revealed to me the profound connection between the quality of our health and our relationships. This insight has motivated me, over the past twelve years, to research the secrets of optimum health as a foundation for lasting love.

These are health secrets that are generally not explored in medical school. In medical school, doctors are indoctrinated into the culture of examining the symptoms, identifying the sickness, and prescribing a drug to treat that sickness. They learn very little about how to be healthy or to sustain successful relationships.

There are no university courses entitled "Better Nutrition For Better Sex". Drugs sometimes save lives, but they also have negative side effects that do little to preserve the passion in a relationship. Ideally, drugs should be used as a last resort and 90 % of our health plan should be drug free. From this perspective, the heath care crisis, as well as our high rate of divorce in America, is indirectly caused by our dependence on doctors and prescription drugs.

Most people have not even considered that taking prescribed drugs (even for the small stuff) can weaken their relationships, which in turn makes them more vulnerable to more disease. For example, if you are feeling depressed or anxious, a drug may numb your pain, but it does nothing to help you correct the cause of your problem. It can even prevent you from feeling your natural motivation to get the emotional support you need. In a variety of ways, our common health complaints are all expressions of two major conditions: our lack of education to identify and support unmet gender-specific emotional needs; and our lack of education to identify and support unmet gender-specific nutritional needs.

With an understanding of natural solutions that have been around for thousands of years, drugs are not needed to treat many common complaints. Some symptoms like low energy, weight gain, allergies, hormonal imbalance, mood swings, poor sleep, indigestion, lack of focus, ADD and ADHD, procrastination, low motivation, memory loss, decreased libido, PMS, vaginal dryness, muscle and joint pain, or the lack of passion in life and/or our relationships can be treated drug-free. By using drugs (even over-the-counter drugs) to treat these common complaints, our bodies and relationships are weakened, making us more vulnerable to bigger and more costly health challenges like cancer, diabetes, heart disease, auto-immune disease, dementia, and Alzheimer's. In simple terms, by handling the easy stuff (the common complaints) without doctors and drugs, we can protect ourselves from the big stuff (cancer, heart disease, dementia, etc.) We can be healthy and also enjoy lasting love and passion in our personal lives.

Even if you are taking anti-depressants or hormone replacement therapy, sometimes all it takes to stop treating the symptom is to directly handle the cause. With specific mineral orotates (something most people have never heard of) or omega three oil from the brains of salmon, your stress levels immediately drop and you begin to feel happy and in love again.

For every health challenge, we have explored the effects on our relationships, with as well as natural remedies that can sometimes produce immediate positive results. You can find these natural solutions to common health complaints for free at my website: www.MarsVenus.com.

What they don't teach in medical school is how to be healthy and happy without the use of drugs or hormone replacement. By refusing drugs and taking responsibility for your health, a wealth of new possibilities can become available to you. We are designed to be healthy and happy, and it is within our reach if we commit to increasing our knowledge.

New research regarding the brain differences in men and women reveals how specific nutritional supplements, combined with gender-specific relationship and self-nurturing skills, can stimulate the hormones of health, happiness and increased energy. Over the past 10 years in my healing center in California, I witnessed how natural solutions coupled with gender-specific relationship skills could solve our common health complaints without drugs. By addressing these common complaints without prescribed drugs, not only do we feel better, but our relationships have the potential to improve dramatically.

Ultimately the cause of all our common complaints is higher stress levels. Researchers around the world all agree that chronic stress levels in our bodies provide a basis for any and all disease to take hold. An easy and quick solution for lowering our stress reactions is specific nutritional support combined with gender-smart relationship skills. Extra nutritional support is needed because stress depletes the body very quickly of essential nutrients. When a car engine is running more quickly, it uses fuel more quickly. When we are stressed, we need both extra nutrients and extra emotional support. Understanding what we need to take and where to get it requires education. Every week day at www.MarsVenus.com I have a live daily show where I freely answer questions and provide this much-needed new gender-specific insight.

At www.MarsVenus.com, we are happy to share what we have learned for creating healthy bodies and positive relationships. You can find a host of natural solutions for common complaints and feel confident that you have the power to feel fully alive with an abundance of energy and positive feelings that will enrich all your relationships.

Bringing Balance to Your Life

DENNIS GARRIDO

When I woke up in the hospital staring up into the terrified eyes of someone I cared about, after my second cardiac arrest in one year, I knew that things had to change in my life. Especially because I was only in my twenties at the time.

Everything in my life was out of balance. Obviously, physically because I was lying in the emergency room, but more importantly my mind, emotions, and spirit were completely out of whack, and that had taken a toll on my body.

Now you may be wondering how someone so young could have had two cardiac arrests before the age of 30? It won't be hard to imagine once I share my story with you. I wish I could tell you that I had a great upbringing, one filled with laughter and love, but it wasn't.

At age eleven I was removed from my parent's home by The Children's Aid Society because they deemed my parents unfit to raise me. During that time, I went through a whirlwind of emotions. A part of me was happy that change was finally occurring, because clearly at that point, the way things were, wasn't working at all.

Another part of me felt fear because of the unknown. I didn't know exactly where I would be living, nor did I know for sure what my group & foster homes would be like, what the other kids would be like, what the living conditions would be like, how far or close I'd be to my family and hometown, etc. Essentially, I wasn't 100% certain nor 100% convinced that I was going into better circumstances.

Also, I felt sad, since I wouldn't see my parents or siblings anymore, nor my home town and many of the people whom I'd see on a regular basis; everything FAMILIAR would be gone! Lastly, I felt angry, that it had come to me being removed from my parent's house, away from those who were in my life for all those years. As twisted and messed up as it may be, I was angry that I was leaving a life that I had become accustomed to and felt somewhat comfortable in (comfortable in comparison to the unknown that lay ahead); and most of all, angry that I was leaving FAMILIARITY!!!!

Please understand me, I am no longer angry at my parents, and you shouldn't be either. They did the best they could, but when you are broken yourself, unless you find a way out, you will repeat what had been bestowed on you from the previous generations. I can be thankful because what I went through helped create the person I am today and as a coach, it gives me great empathy and understanding to be able to help others. So, don't feel sorry for me because even though my life had a rough start, I get to choose the rest of it and it is going to be GREAT!!!

THE NEXT SEVEN YEARS OF MY LIFE

For the next seven years until I turned 18, I was bounced from foster/group home to foster/group home. I rarely spent more than three months at any one place, and it caused some major emotional setbacks that took me a long time to overcome.

One of the biggest negative emotional setbacks was again to do with familiarity. As I spent time with those at my new home, seeing them every day and coming to know them personally; I naturally formed a connection/ friendship with them. It seemed that no sooner had I done that; they were removed from my life. People whom I really liked (a few of them, whom I loved), ALL GONE!!! Which basically solidified my already ingrained defence mechanism of keeping distant from others; not allowing anyone to get close enough to form any connection with me.

Inevitably, this made it very difficult for me to form any type of relationship with anyone. School and extracurricular activities were hard because I never knew how long I would be staying in one place. What was the point of making friends if I could never keep them? It was a lot easier to keep my distance than to reach out yet again and have everything torn away from me.

Eventually, I started to tear down the wall that prevented me from getting too close to anyone. To this day, the negative emotional setbacks I experienced, still affect me to some degree; though I CHOOSE not to allow them to prevent me from forming meaningful relationships!

THE DARKEST TIME OF MY LIFE

All that change led to one of the darkest periods of my life. Emotionally and mentally I had shut down and could no longer function. Life was so hard. Even things that were simple, now became agonizingly difficult and it hit the point where I didn't want to live anymore. What was the use of carrying on in this horrible life when there wasn't any hope of it changing?

My life began to narrow down to one permanent solution, and that was to end it all by committing suicide. I just couldn't handle life anymore, but I truly believe that Almighty God, the universe or whatever you want to call it, had a bigger plan for me. Even though I tried several times, I just couldn't die!!! Because of those attempts, I ended up in psychiatric institutions, a few times.

It finally came to the point where I was tired of trying to die, I was tired of institutions and I was weary from all the self-harm, and so I came to a decision. I guess you could say that it was a turning point in my life; I wasn't going to attempt suicide anymore. I wasn't sure what to do because my circumstances hadn't changed, but I was willing to look for options. That was the beginning point of change in my life. The will to live!!!

IT DIDN'T GET BETTER RIGHT AWAY

Life is a journey with twists, hills, and valleys of varying shapes and sizes, with occasional points where you make decisions that put you on a different path. The determination not to kill myself had set me on a new road, but I still didn't know what to do or which way to go. It was slow going as I fumbled my way through, but at least I was moving forward!!!

At age 18 I was no longer in the custody of The Children's Aid Society, so, I moved back with my parents, which was the perfect testing grounds for me to apply the life lessons I had learned so far. You would be amazed by how much maturity one can have at 18 when you have been through what I have. It wasn't easy, and it was hard work, but I managed to re-establish a relationship with my parents and not only complete high school, but also graduate from post-secondary schooling.

One of the things I had decided to do was get my student loans paid off in the six-month grace period, which I managed to do; but in doing so, I pushed myself way beyond my physical limits which brought on the first cardiac arrest.

You would think I would have learned from that first experience, but I didn't, and less than a year later we are back to the beginning of this chapter waking up in the hospital from my second one.

This time I learned my lesson and chose a different path, but I still didn't know how to achieve what I needed. For so long I had lived in imbalance, that I didn't know where to start, but the catalyst for change was just around the corner.

I FINALLY REALIZED WHAT BALANCE WAS

Believe it or not, it is the simplest things that can bring about the most profound changes in life. My search for balance in my life had begun, and it is amazing how the answer came; by a knock at my door one day.

That day I was busy working on something, so when the first knock came, I ignored it. It was only after a couple of rings of the doorbell that I finally decided that I would answer it. There was a well-dressed gentleman at the door and even though I don't remember most of what he said, one thing became clear, I was missing an essential element to finding the balance I craved. Now, I knew what it was. You can only find balance when you address ALL the areas of your life, and I had been missing one. The spiritual side.

It is amazing what happens when you finally have all the pieces together. As I started to study the Bible, I finally could build a solid spiritual foundation, that enabled me to re-evaluate things in my life, and thus, put a plan together to create balance in my life. In the rest of this chapter, I am going to share with you what I learned.

Just before I do that, I do want to mention one thing. All of this is a process. Can I say that I am 100% balanced in my life? No, but when I started at 3-4% and then jumped to 85%, I think that is very good growth. It's difficult to attain 100% balance in every aspect of one's life, that is why even the most successful people keep learning and growing. So, the goal is not perfection, but growth. As long as you are continuing to move forward, that is all that matters.

7 STEPS TO BRING BALANCE TO YOUR LIFE

Here's one of the things that I have learned about bringing balance to your life. In some ways, it is easy. The steps I am going to teach you are simple to understand. The hard part is training yourself to be aware of it every day and live by it. The good thing is, though it may be hard at first, the more you practice it, the easier it gets.

STEP 1

Ask yourself, "What are my priorities in life?" You want to look at it from all aspects of your life, personal and professional. In terms of personal that includes goals physically, emotionally, mentally, spiritually, relationships (such as your spouse or significant other), family and friends. You want to look at it from the point of what you need and what you want. For each one, you should have one to two priorities.

In terms of professional, they can include your current work situation and areas of improvement there, plus plan for your future. Put down both needs and wants.

	NEEDS	WANTS
P E R S O N A L		
P R O F E S S I O N A L		

STEP 2

Look at your needs column. What are the most important priorities personally and professionally? It is important that you only start out working on a few at a time. If you try to do everything at once, you will become overwhelmed and quit. Then, figure out the things you need to do to get those needs met.

STEP 3

Now go through your wants and do the same thing as Step 2 above. Don't overlook this. Part of having balance in life is having both your needs and wants met. Obviously, your needs are more important, but without the wants, you give up hope.

STEP 4

Set up a timeline for those needs to be accomplished. What are you going to do today, this week, this month, this year, and in the next five years to bring yourself to reach those priorities?

STEP 5

Do the same thing for your wants. Set up your timeline of completion.

STEP 6

DO THE ACTIONS. Here is where the rubber meets the road. You can plan and plan and plan, but if there is no action involved you will be in the same place, with the same problems, five years from now.

STEP 7

Re-evaluate. Every few months go back through this whole process again.

As you grow and change, so will your priorities, your needs and your wants.

THE BEST WAY TO ACCOMPLISH THIS

Very rarely can a person accomplish this alone. Have you ever heard the saying, "You can't see the forest for the trees?" That is what happens in our lives. We get so caught up in the unimportant things right in front of us, that we miss the big picture and we don't recognize growth when it occurs.

Now, you do have several options. One is to have family members try to help you through this. While you do need their support, they are usually looking at the same trees you are and can miss things.

Two, you can go to friends for help. They do tend to see more of the big picture, but many times they can't give you the encouragement and motivation you need at times to get past yourself.

Three, you work with a professional who knows how to help you bring balance to your life. They can come alongside of you and guide you to the quickest path to success because there will be obstacles that try to stop you. Did I forget to mention that?

No road to balance is smooth; little pebbles will get into your shoes to irritate you and take your focus off your goals. Barriers will be put up that you will have to learn how to go over, under, around or through. People will get in your way and tell you that it is the wrong road to take and you should follow them. All sorts of things will try to keep you from what you want.

Coaches are keen observers who can not only help you with what is going on right now, but they have been down your road and they know what is up ahead and can keep you moving forward, even when everything is telling you to stop.

That is what I'm offering to be for you. Let me help you on your path to balance in your life. I have been on both sides of the coin, and I can guide you through the roughest parts. I can relate to what you are feeling and am more than willing to help you navigate this wonderful thing called life.

First of all, if you would like more information on how to start this process, you can pre-order my upcoming book at www.dennisgarrido.com Second, you can email me at dennis@dennisgarrido.com and request your free 15-minute phone consultation where we can discuss your situation and see if we are a good fit for each other. Third, maybe you realize more people need to hear this message. I am also available to speak to groups and conferences. If so, just send me an email, and we can arrange a time to speak.

No matter what you decide, know this. You can achieve balance in your life. It is possible. I can tell you that it has been worth everything I went through to get to this point. The peace I experience now, compared to the chaos I lived before, is so amazing and I wish the same for you.

Don't miss out. Make the choice to change your life today, and I guarantee that you won't regret it!!!

Motivation Does Activate and Sustain Behaviour

How to Bring Results in Life and Business

JULIE HOGBIN

Before we talk about motivation in any great detail, it would be a good idea to cover the basics about what motivation really is. There are many, many, theories and huge amounts of research has been conducted on the subject over many decades. To be honest, with all the information out there it can be confusing as to what it all means.

One thing is for sure, one theory — one piece of information — does not cover it all as each researcher has their own bent and interpretation on the subject. It is when you are able to link it all together that it starts to make sense and you are able to do something with the information to help yourself.

I have researched, read about, practiced, and taught this subject to over 20,000 Leaders in Life, Business and the Entrepreneur market, both one-on-one and in small groups for very nearly three decades, and I am still learning.

This chapter is based around my knowledge, my interpretation, and a definition of Motivation that I have worked with for a long time. I have neither found nor developed a better definition — yet!

"Motivation is a conscious or unconscious driving force that arouses and directs action towards the achievement of a desired goal."

ClaimYourDestiny.global   #ConsciousLeadership

So, what does this mean in reality? It means that we are motivated by internal and external factors and that sometimes we know what those factors are and sometimes we don't: Our actions and thoughts are both conscious and unconscious in nature. It also means that the motives provoke a reaction and an action that help us 'get' something we want — a goal — and as a driving force they are powerful.

So my 1st questions to you are:

- What is your goal?

- What are you working towards?

- How many goals do you have?

- What is driving you?

- How conscious are you?

Motivation is an internal force; we are the only ones who can motivate us. Motivation can be affected by external influences. Ultimately it is us, and only us, that make the decision to do or not to do something. Nobody can make you feel or do anything! It is your absolute choice to capitulate and do, or to resist and not do.

We make the decision based on the information we have at the time and how confident we feel. There are many emotions and personal characteristics that come into play when we are talking about motivation and all that entails.

When we say that others motivate us what it really means is that they have created an environment that inspires us to do something. We make the decision out of fear in some cases, because we know it makes sense in other cases, because we aspire to be like the individual, or, more simply, just because we want to.

For you, and everybody else, your desired goal always provides you with a positive outcome. It gives you something you want even if that want is unconsciously driven. For others viewing it from their perspective, that outcome may be viewed as negative.

Let me explain what I mean with a couple of examples.

Addicts of any description do whatever it takes to fuel their need. They are achieving their desired outcome with more alcohol, more food, less food, more drugs, or just more of something, and they will go to extreme lengths to get it, such as selling personal and other people's belongings, lying and deceiving, going into debt and stealing.

Someone comes home with great intent of doing some research, maybe to write a book or to do some personal development such as going to the gym, and they end up sitting in front of the TV for hours with a bottle of wine. What is their driving force? We may not understand it as the viewer but there is definitely one for the person being observed.

Let's look at a couple of positive examples with a more generally accepted encouraging outcome.

A young person decides what they want to achieve in their life. They study like crazy to get the grades required to get to the top university and to study in a class of four with the top professor in their subject matter field, and they achieve it.

An individual from an underprivileged background wants to change their life, achieve greater things than have ever been achieved in their family, and become independently wealthy, and they are successful in achieving their goals.

Now for every example shared the opposite can be true as well. Not everybody becomes an addict, not everyone slouches in front of the TV, not every student achieves their potential, and not every underprivileged individual becomes independently wealthy.

"Everything you do is goal-driven. Everything you do is because you want the end result — whatever that end result may be!"

ClaimYourDestiny.global   #ConsciousLeadership

The examples are all based on how motivated the individual is to achieve their goal. Now if you know your goal consciously, can keep it in focus and resist the temptation of your old ways, you can achieve marvellous results.

The rest of this chapter will look at what drives you and how you can change your habits and behaviours over a period both short and long term, with the aim to achieve whatever it is you want.

I reference no theory in this chapter. There are many to read and learn which are of use to us all intellectually and unless the theory is practically applied and interpreted into reality all they remain are theories. I have spent decades interpreting theories into real life behaviours that make a difference for the better.

A few more questions for you to think about first.

- What are your drivers?

- What are your values?

- What is your risk tolerance?

- How much do you want to fit in with the 'norm' of your social group?

- How much do you really want, on a scale of 1 to 10, the thing it is you are aiming to achieve?

- How comfortable are you with change?

There are a lot more questions to ask but these will start you on the journey to understand your own motivators.

"Your motives create your habits, for good and bad, as they are your driving force."

ClaimYourDestiny.global   #ConsciousLeadership

There is so much information coming at us on a minute by minute basis. We make thousands upon thousands of decisions every day — so many in fact, we cannot be conscious of all the decisions, to do or not to do something, that we do make. We would be completely overwhelmed if we did.

So what do we do? We create patterns of behaviour that we do not have to think about, as it is quicker that way, to achieve our outcomes. We create habits that get us what we want in the easiest manner.

"Your habits have created your behaviour through your values, beliefs, and attitudes."

ClaimYourDestiny.global   #ConsciousLeadership

HABITS

Habits are a set of thoughts, behaviours, and ways of being that are developed through repeated behaviour. Habits are formed from the moment we become aware that there is a 'norm' of how to do things. Some we pick up from our parents, guardians, siblings, and influential individuals around us at a very early age. Others we develop for ourselves through the maturing process.

"Look to your parents for your beliefs about the world and yourself – you may be amazed at the similarities."

ClaimYourDestiny.global   #ConsciousLeadership

Once habits are created they can be difficult to break. To break a habit, we must consciously think about doing something different and then do it — which can equal hard work and being uncomfortable.

The thing is, we can all break habits if we really want to. BUT (and there is a big BUT) the unconscious part of our being is there to keep us safe. Any change and it may feel we are under threat and revert quickly to the old ways.

"Talk to your unconscious and ask its permission if you want to change some deep held habits and motivations to do things in a new way."

"Sounds a bit weird? Well it works, try it for yourself."

ClaimYourDestiny.global   #ConsciousLeadership

VALUES

Your values are a central part of who you are and who you want to be. By becoming more aware of these driving motivators in your life, you can use them as a guide to make the best choice in any situation.

Your decisions and actions, when in line with your values, will be easy to make and put into practice. If you are attempting to do something that is not held as a value to you, you will find it harder to do and, potentially, you will be in conflict with yourself.

Here is an example. If one of your values is honesty and you are in a relationship, business or personal, with someone who you know tells untruths, how hard will you find it to trust them? What will this do to your behaviour and your motivation within the relationship?

Values can be worked with, reordered, and installed — so do not lose hope. I personally have needed to work hard on my value regarding money. To say the least, it was slightly askew!

ATTITUDES

Your attitude is a predisposition to respond either negatively or positively towards an idea, object, person, or situation. It is the way you feel about something or someone. It can also be a particular feeling or opinion. It is seen as a conscious behaviour but will come from an unconscious driver.

Your attitude evolves as a result of your beliefs and values and will influence:

- Your choice of action and behaviour

- Your response to challenges

- Your response to incentives

- Your response to a word

- Your response to someone trying to help you

We all have an attitude — we cannot not have one. Generally, when it is said someone has an attitude it is meant as a negative opinion, but attitudes are drivers for good as well. It is just a common adaptation of a word which is more often linked to negativity.

As with anything else we do, our attitude is a choice we make. My choice, and I trust yours as you are reading this book, is to start each day with a positive attitude — it soon becomes a habit.

If you want to change something in your life, surround yourself with those who are on the same path or learn from those who have already done the 'thing' that you want to do. Attitudes are contagious so eradicate those personally held by yourself and those that are owned by people that may be in your circle who aren't helping you. If you don't know what your attitudes are, ask someone for feedback who will tell you the truth.

Also carefully study your close associates to make your own decisions on who stays with you on your journey and who leaves, their attitudes can be contagious. Look at the relationships that are in your life and acknowledge whether they are supporting you or hindering you. Decisions then can be made from a realistic position of what you want to do.

SOCIAL INTELLIGENCE

Social intelligence indicates that portions of our knowledge acquisition can be directly related to observing others within the context of social interactions, experiences and media influences.

So what does this mean to all of us? Basically, it means that if we see something that is rewarded, we copy it so that we get rewarded. We achieve the same result as we have observed, therefore we have achieved our result, which was our goal. There is far more to it but that's the basic concept. We learn by example from others.

So who do we copy? We copy those close to us and we adopt behaviours to fit into the crowd and belong. As we get older, we copy those who we admire or those who we aspire to be like. We develop a sense of self and become more aware of what it is we want. We begin to lead rather than follow — well some of us do and I expect you are a leader since you are reading this book! Join my Facebook group for more, https://www.facebook.com/groups/ClaimYourDestiny/

We are motivated to belong to a group with a certain set of characteristics.

That could be because it is what we want or it can be because we know no different. It can be through peer pressure or choice, but whichever route we take it is ultimately our choice!

Join my Facebook group for more, https://www.facebook.com/groups/ClaimYourDestiny/

It is these drivers of behaviour that make you act differently from, or the same as, others in any given situation. So, by understanding these drivers, you can better understand why you do the things you do. The skill is not only to understand your conscious needs, but also those that are unconscious in nature.

"In the choice between changing one's mind and proving there's no need to do so, most people get busy on the proof."

– John Kenneth Galbraith

SELF-PERCEPTION

Self-perception is the belief or disbelief in our own capabilities to achieve a goal or an outcome. These beliefs provide the foundation for human motivation, well-being, and personal accomplishment. This is because unless you believe that your actions can produce the outcomes you desire, you will have little incentive to act or to persevere in the face of difficulties.

Of course, human functioning is influenced by many factors. The success or failure you experience as you engage the countless tasks that comprise your life naturally influences the many decisions you must make. Also, the knowledge and skills you possess will certainly play critical roles in what you choose to do and not do.

"People's level of motivation, emotional states, and actions are based more on what they believe than on what is objectively true. For this reason, how you behave can often be better predicted by the beliefs you hold about your capabilities than by what you are actually capable of accomplishing."

ClaimYourDestiny.global   #ConsciousLeadership

You only need to watch one of the reality TV shows to see how clearly some people are deluded about their own abilities. The opposite is also true — you talk to someone who you know is gifted and they think and believe the complete opposite.

Our upbringing and early influencers, or even a recent happening, have a huge part to play in how and what we believe about ourselves. The great news though is whatever has happened in the past does not have to happen in our future.

These perceptions help determine what you do with the knowledge and skills you have. They also explain why your behaviours are sometimes not matched to your actual capabilities and why your behaviour may differ widely from somebody else, even when you have similar knowledge and skills.

For example, many talented people suffer frequent (and sometimes debilitating) bouts of self-doubt about capabilities they clearly possess, just as many individuals are confident about what they can accomplish despite possessing a modest repertoire of skills. Belief and reality are seldom perfectly matched, and individuals are typically guided by their beliefs when they engage the world.

As a consequence, your accomplishments are generally better predicted by your self-perception than by your previous achievements, knowledge, or skills. Of course, no amount of confidence or self-appreciation can produce success when requisite skills and knowledge are absent.

"Skills and knowledge can all be gained if you want them enough and you find the right mentor to teach you."

ClaimYourDestiny.global   #ConsciousLeadership

COLLECTIVE PERCEPTION

Because individuals operate collectively as well as individually, self-perception is both a personal and a social construct. Collective systems develop a sense of collective effectiveness, it can create the group's shared belief in its capability to attain goals and accomplish desired tasks.

One brain is one but the collective brainpower of a group equals more than the sum of its parts — it's the adage $1+1=3$ or $2+2 = 5$. However, this is only true when the collective works together in harmony with the same aim. If members of the collective are working against each other one brain doesn't even equate to one — it will function at a lesser capability, as will the individual as they will be experiencing conflict.

For example, organisations develop collective beliefs about the capability of their salesforce to perform, of their managers to teach and otherwise enhance the lives of their workforce, and of their administrators and policymakers to create environments conducive to these tasks. Organisations, as well as individuals, also create beliefs that are not positive — they cannot gain additional sales, clients, revenue, etc. Collectiveness creates a culture which needs to be managed.

Organisations with a strong sense of positive collective perception exercise empowering and vitalising influences over their employees. These effects are evident in their results.

The power of others' attitudes (as mentioned previously) are contagious and will affect your motivation. If you are in the company of a high sender of negative emotion, you will be affected. If you are in the company of a high sender of positivity, it will be less influential.

As the saying goes, it only takes one bad apple to spoil the barrel.

Weed out the bad apples and your motivation will improve. Take on more of the good apples that are doing the same thing that you want to do and your motivation will improve by leaps and bounds.

CHOICES

Only you can justify the choices you make and most of you will make your choices in reference to past experiences rather than future opportunities. Change how you think and you will change your future.

"The definition of insanity is doing the same thing over and over again and expecting a different result."

– Albert Einstein

How do you change to get a different result? It's easy, think differently and take different actions. Open your mind and your being to possibilities; your past does not have to equal your future. With #ConsciousLeadership it can all change.

Every thought, every action, and every decision you make takes you closer to, or further away, from where you want to be. The smallest of decisions compounded over time creates massive change. Rather than attempt to make a huge change overnight, which can be scary and overwhelming, make small incremental changes that lead you towards your goal.

What do I mean? 5 minutes exercise a day wont make much difference if you do or don't do it BUT 5 minutes everyday will. A cake on one day wont make much difference to your health BUT a cake every day will (in the wrong direction). Delaying cutting the lawn for one day wont make much difference BUT delaying every day will.

Even doing nothing takes you further away because everything else is moving forward. The skills of yesteryear will not suffice in the next year. Think about how technology changes. If you haven't kept up with the last change you will soon be a very long way behind!

Sometimes, it can be a life-changing event that allows you to make the decision to do something immediately that you have tried before and failed at. A friend of mine, when diagnosed with cancer, stopped smoking overnight after 40 years. Please do not leave it until that type of thing happens before you change. Take on board #ConsciousLeadership now and change your life for the better, it is your choice!

Start to work now on different decisions for what you want and need:

- Why wait to be taken through a disciplinary process at work before you improve your skills or performance?

- Why wait until you are so over or underweight before you change your nutrition intake?

- Why wait until you cannot walk upstairs without puffing before you increase your fitness level?

- Why wait until you are close to retirement to think about how much money you need to live on and enjoy your retirement?

Through reading, applying, and practicing the experiences of others, you can learn what has worked for those before you, and you can apply those principles in your own life.

Motivational states are directive, they guide behaviours toward satisfying specific goals or specific needs. Do you have clearly defined goals? If you don't, sit down now, identify what it is you really want or need, and write that down. Then create a plan of how you will achieve it. This will provide you with motivation to do things differently.

If you want more information on how to this, I can highly recommend my book 'The Life Changing Magic of Setting Goals'. It is available from Amazon or through ClaimYourDestiny.global

"Change begins with your awareness that your beliefs are a choice; all beliefs, conscious or unconscious, are based on a choice."

ClaimYourDestiny.global   #ConsciousLeadership

There are a myriad of choices to be made all of the time. If you choose a different way to do something, gather information that allows you to make an educated choice for action. Do your research and due diligence and pick the best solution for you.

This will enhance your confidence, create new knowledge, quieten the inner doubting voice, match your values, enhance your beliefs, or question them to bolster your attitude.

This will allow you to convince your unconscious that you are looking after it and it will help you. Provide your unconscious with the reason why you are making alternate choices to that of the past and it will support you all the way.

DELAYED GRATIFICATION

There have been many studies done related to the benefits of delayed gratification. What does this really mean? It means living with the future in mind rather than the present.

In this world of instant gratification, keeping up with the Joneses, wearing the right designer labels, being influenced by adverts that say you must have this face cream and that aftershave, feeling like your holidays must become bigger and more expensive, having to change your car every two years, etc. It can be hard to resist the instant temptation, to be outside the norm, or to exclude yourself from your friends' activities.

In the moment, sometimes it can seem obvious to take the reward, and worry about the future in the future.

Your choice is dependent on your goals, your drivers, your beliefs (and how strong they are), and how strong your will to resist temptation is.

If you can recognise when you have an opportunity for a larger or more important reward, it shows you know the difference between your needs and your wants. When you can recognise these situations, there are key terms you must think of.

Patience, will, and self-control are all characteristics of people who are masters of their environment. One common challenge is postponing immediate gratification in the pursuit of long-term goals. Delayed gratification is the process of transcending immediate temptations to achieve long-term goals.

Knowing how to create, manage, and control your goals is the first step towards completing the things you want most in life; with a goal, we engage our brain to work toward it.

Think of goals as roadmaps designed to keep you on target. They make the experience and the journey possible and more enjoyable. They, in fact, become priorities that drive our actions. They become motivators.

Let me ask you once again:

• What are your long-term goals? And for some of you

• What are your short-term goals?

If you do not have goals sit down now and plan them for yourself, tell yourself and others they are important, write them down and believe you are worthy of them and you will achieve them. Focus on them and they will become a reality

THE POWER OF QUESTIONS

Questions, when constructed in the right way, are the most powerful way to access your beliefs. And this works irrespective of who asks the question. Ask yourself a question and your mind will do its best to provide you with an answer. The better your question, the better the answer.

Do you want to spend the rest of your life figuring out how to get the things you desire, or would you rather put all the guesswork behind you and get down to the fun of building an out-of-this-world lifestyle? Easy choice, right? Then do yourself a favour: suspend your disbelief, lower your shields, and try a simple way of improving your life.

Identify someone you respect who's already experiencing what you're after, find out what questions they habitually ask themselves to achieve those experiences, then use those questions yourself.

This is a globally powerful approach to success that can get you the things you want more quickly than anything else I've discovered. The habitual questions that others ask themselves when asked by yourself, to yourself can transform your life. You don't even need to understand how it all works really, although the answer's quite simple:

"When you change your habitual questions, you change your beliefs, when you change your beliefs, you change your actions, when you change your actions you change your results."

ClaimYourDestiny.global #ConsciousLeadership

Try it! Take the time to prove to yourself that it works, that it can change the level of pain and pleasure in your life. If you like the results, keep using the questions you've discovered until they become second nature. Do this and you won't care about the why's and the wherefore's. You'll be too busy! You'll have learned firsthand there's nothing more powerful than a good question followed by action.

Ask different questions, and you will end up thinking different thoughts, saying different words, taking different actions, and getting different results. When you go one step further by modeling the questions of successful people, you're helping to ensure that the different results you're pursuing are also good results. In other words, you've done everything you can to arrive at a different place — a good place — to develop different beliefs, which are also profitable beliefs, and to become a different person who is more like the people you admire.

FOCUS

So what does all this mean really?

It means that by looking at why you do what you do and the beliefs behind that, you can basically change the thoughts and motives that direct your behaviour so that you achieve a different result, start a new job, get a promotion, create your own business, leave a relationship, start a relationship, have that difficult conversation, learn to swim, fly a plane, or simply eat a new food; the list is endless.

It is your choice completely — where your focus goes your energy flows — so change your focus to change your results.

Some of our important choices have a timeline. If you delay a decision, the opportunity is gone forever. Sometimes your doubts will stop you from making a choice that involves change and an opportunity may be missed. If you really truly want to change, start now — now is as good a time as any.

Create and ClaimYourDestiny.global through #ConsciousLeadership

My Facebook page and group is ClaimYourDestiny or you can follow me on Twitter @JulieHogbin. Visit ClaimYourDestiny.global for more articles and up to date information, plus various other social media channels and Linkedin. My hashtag is #ConsciousLeadership if you would like to find me.

Motives and motivation are a matter of choice — yours! Choose well, look at why you believe what you believe, and question it. Listen to the answers of the questions you ask and you will create a different future if you really want to.

My final questions to you are:

- How much do you want to change?

- How willing are you to do what is required?

- What do you need to do right now?

Good luck with whatever it is you want to do. Here's to your fabulous success; you know where to find me.

Julie xx

A Dream Life for the Asking

TOM BARBER

There is an enchanting transformation that occurs during those fleeting moments between sleeping and waking as you emerge out of a deep, relaxed slumber before the demands of the day come tumbling into your conscious world. It is also a magical moment of pure potentiality that contains seeds of inspiration or a solution to that insolvable problem that has hounded you for days. Just as you're about to reach out for that breakthrough thought (the one that teeters on the edge of your consciousness), the alarm clock rings, your smartphone dings a text message alert, your baby cries or your dog bays for food. You lose that thread of inspiration; it's gone as if it never existed.

Have you experienced those moments when you say, "But I just had it in my head, it was *right* there!" only to realize that creativity has tenuously slipped through your fingers?

What if you were able to access this state of pure potentiality as often as you wanted to, when you wanted to? You may require some expert assistance in the beginning to reprogram your beliefs so that you know it is, indeed, possible. However, once you've exercised your "mental muscles" and familiarised your mind and body often enough to get the process fully, you will be able to tap into this infinite source of creativity, inspiration, solutions and possibility at will. What if you could access this untapped power for health, greater happiness and contentment, and for peak performance and success, as if it were "second nature"? Well, you can.

Hypnosis is the technology I use to usher people into deep trance states where they can connect to their inner power. Coined by James Braid, a 19th century Scottish surgeon, the term hypnosis comes from "Hypnos," the Greek god of sleep. You don't fall asleep during hypnosis, however; instead you enter a state of deep, calm relaxation during which you can work directly with your subconscious, that part of your mind that takes care of everything behind the scenes.

Back to that moment in the morning, when you're woken up by the barking of your dogs. From that point on, your conscious mind takes over; it goes through the checklist of what you've got to do during the day, the meetings you've got to attend, the chat you're going to have with your boss or travel plans you're going to make for your next vacation. It seems as if the conscious mind is calling the shots, but actually the subconscious mind is continually doing all the hard work.

It is the subconscious that keeps the heart beating, and that tells your lungs to keep pumping oxygen, which speeds up the movement of your legs as a car is threatening to run you down while you are crossing the street. When you cut yourself, you don't think logically to yourself, "Okay, time for the blood to clot now and the white cells to come fight off infection!" All these seemingly simple, yet intricate reactions are silently and efficiently orchestrated by the powerful subconscious. Think of it as your life's Control Panel.

The pure power of the subconscious is revealed in fleeting moments all the time, even when you're asleep. We're just not always aware it's happening. When you've had a stroke of inspiration, or the genius of an idea, that moment of "divine aha!" leaps out like a Jack-in-the-box, released into your conscious mind. The latter is often met, however, with the vast amounts of data, external stimuli, emotions and physical experiences that are part of your interaction with the world from moment to moment. The trick is to keep the genius intact and to expand its reality within your conscious world. You can learn how to do that too.

The subconscious is the seat of imagination, impulse, creativity and emotion and is also the storehouse of your memories, which means it's one mighty big reservoir. Tapping into it at will and harnessing its power can be truly awesome.

SO WHAT DOES IT ALL MEAN?

What does all this have to do with hypnosis? How can it reveal to us such inner power? Hypnosis takes you to that relaxed state, where your brain frequency literally slows down. Your subconscious mind can then come to the front of the stage as the headline act and revel in the spotlight. In a hypnotic trance state, you remain alert, but you're incredibly focused, just as if you were fully engaged in a really good book or a compelling movie. You switch off external stimuli and are fully engaged in the world of the book or film as if you were right there, in the story.

Hypnosis gives you the key to open the door to the subconscious, access its amazing wealth of information, creativity and resources. It allows you to "anchor" a positive mindset and feelings to be accessed at any point in the future. In this manner, you gain distinct control of your emotions and can manage your mindset for positive behaviour, essentially creating the outcomes you've only ever dreamed of before.

Let's take an example. Let's say you almost drowned when you were a little kid and have since avoided the water. Now an adult, every time you approach the sea, you have a plunging feeling in your stomach. You feel left out on beach holidays because you're afraid of being too close to the water; you don't even dip a toe in the swimming pool. However, you've fallen in love with a marine biologist and you feel that there's something missing if you can't share the love of being in the water with your new partner. Are you always going to stay on the sidelines, or are you going to engage with life so you can have endless fun and build great memories with the love of your life? Which would you choose?

You've been dominated by fear surrounding the bad experience but, with hypnosis, I can take away the sting of the anxiety and terror, as well as any undesirable thoughts that creep into your mind unwillingly at the sight of the ocean. Then, I can help you replace those unhappy memories with a new, more desirable set of emotions and sensory experiences. I can explore with you any feelings of fun, delight and sharing that you've encountered previously in doing something else, like playing football or cooking with friends, and link those feelings with being in the water. By taking these steps, we would together reprogram your mind-body connection so that it reacts positively to swimming and everything associated with it, such as soaking up the warm sun, feeling the breeze, tasting the salt in the water, thriving in the adventure and, ultimately, enjoying more intimate love!

To ensure you can re-access this desirable state, I use a technique called Clenched Fist Auto Anchoring to make sure that these positive emotions are powerfully stored in your body's memory. By anchoring this sensory experience and all its powerfully positive benefits that are meaningful to *you*, it ensures that you can retrieve or spark happy feelings and sensations around water any time you want, in any situation, at will.

Together, through hypnosis, we will have moved you from a previously inhibiting fear to a pleasurable and fearless sense of freedom and adventure. Your whole world will have just changed immeasurably. This is just one example of how well hypnosis works; it is effective in all situations, from helping you pass your driving exam to overcoming your anxiety around public speaking to surmounting weight problems, habits and low-esteem, to finding your life's purpose and creating great success beyond your wildest dreams.

BELIEVE YOU DESERVE MORE, GET MORE

Hypnotherapy is a powerful technology, and it changes lives. The first step forward begins with *you*.

Ask yourself…

- Do you feel that your life could be better lived?
- Do you long to contribute more positively to your family, your friends, your customers and to the world at large?
- Do you feel frustrated because you don't know which direction to take?

- Are you just plain stuck and unwilling to get out of the hole?
- Do you feel there's a vision inside you waiting to be birthed, but you don't know what it is?

The good news is that you'll never have to live another day feeling "less than" or empty, or thinking you're incompetent, unworthy or undeserving. As long as you believe that positive change is possible, that you deserve more than what you're getting right now and that you are capable of great achievements and deeds, positive change is not only possible, it's yours for the taking. What you need now is *the how*.

Hypnosis addresses that "how," that all-important nourishing factor that creates the changes you desire. It's not "if" you can change, but "how" we are going to do this. In my 20 years of experience as a highly qualified psychotherapist using hypnosis and Neuro-Linguistic Programming (NLP), and through my continuing studying and questing, I've found what I believe to be the essential essence that creates the magical moment of true potential where the hypnotic transformation can effortlessly evolve.

The key lies with the ability of one human being to connect with another as well as being deeply attuned to the knowledge and skills inextricably linked to the hypnotic encounter. This is what allows me to connect to the remarkable depth of experience and human-ness of the person who sits by my side. It's about having a true desire to guide you simply through your journey of change, fully believing you can change, even when, right in that moment, your belief is wavering.

Your connection and trust *will* shape and influence the depth of inner journeying, the quality of your therapist's language *will* impact the speed at which you arrive at your desirable state of being, and his or her ultimate belief and faith that change is yours for the taking will impact your ability to access these positive experiences in the future. This I have seen many, many times.

Within myself, I have uncovered the ability to create deep levels of connection with my clients at lightning fast speed, allowing change to happen seamlessly, where extraordinary shifts are open for those who want to achieve, with definitively measurable results. Through my work with many thousands of clients and students, I have harnessed an ability to quickly "feel' where someone is at, to understand how to navigate around their inner terrain and to engage their trust. This ignites their own belief that they can change and really take back control of their futures. I completely believe that change is yours for the taking if you are doing the asking. It is this belief that shines through and creates formidable levels of expectation. When this is in place, the path to change is fully open to the methods and techniques of *how*.

I've been privileged to share amazing transformations as I've delivered conferences and workshops around the world in places such as Eastern Europe, China, Russia and Mexico, all via an interpreter. It's truly phenomenal to experience the depth of the human connection that comes to the fore when words no longer offer a possible means of instant communication, creating a profound and unforgettably moving experience as inner change unfolds before our very eyes.

Such learning has really equipped me to *know* how to move past the words of a story to the deep, true thoughts and feelings of another human being longing for things to change. No two clients are the same, so there's no cookie-cutter approach, but I believe in some fundamentals to embody, some skills that crucially lead the way alongside the "how" for this particular, unique human being with more potential than he or she yet knows. And that's my wonderful job, my life and my inspiration!

My passion for healing others, and my unwavering exploration into my world as my own journey unfolds, places me in the unique position of travelling the path that will need to be walked for this journey of life to evolve further for you too. I've climbed the mountain before, and I know the track well, so I can guide the people I work with from where they are now to where they want to be. And, if they aren't sure about where that is, I can help them locate just what that destination point is too.

My decision to become a therapist fanned an inner flame, which I hadn't known existed, to learn the art of helping others and changing lives. As I engaged in helping others, I found that I tapped into another joy, learning the depths of myself, discovering my inner undiscovered dimensions, becoming freer and more engaged with life and my healing practices. And so the journey continues to unfold.

LIVING A LIFE TO BE PROUD OF

Those are some of the benefits I would like to pass on to you. You see, there is so much that we can do … and so much that you can do too. You can learn to self-hypnotise for those times when you have no access to a trained therapist, so you can harness your tremendous personal power and live a life of which you are proud.

You might be surprised to discover that you *already* self-hypnotise. We all do. Driving to work and being oblivious of your journey, watching TV and losing track of the plot, finding yourself daydreaming out of the office window. These are all examples of drifting into a state of hypnosis. Imagine learning what you can do with that!

Think about the customs that sports teams go through before a big game – the pre-game rituals and the pep talks that are meant to pump up the team and strike fear in the hearts of the opponents.

In the formidable game of rugby, my all-time passion, the New Zealand All Blacks like to take the temperature up a notch and intimidate the competition by performing the Haka, the traditional Maori dance. It involves loud war cries, heavy pounding of feet, stylised gestures of violence, fierce facial expressions with hanging tongues and glowering stares, all barely feet away from the competing team. Yet, the purpose is not just to frighten off the opposing players; the gestures and stomping are a means of "hypnotising" themselves into states where they are strong, fierce and powerful. It is a means by which they tap into the legendary courage of the Maori warriors of old.

So, a dream life is yours for the asking. If you believe you can have an expanded life with more creativity, more accomplishments, more freedom and more passion, if you believe you can be more aligned, the "how" is right there in your hands. It really is within your reach and your grasp. I invite you to walk the path with me, and would be honoured to be your companion in growth.

Once Tom Barber discovered hypnotherapy, he found himself reinvigorated and re-engaged with life, soon desiring to help others as he was himself helped. He has become a leading Hypnotherapist and Psychotherapist helping people to make changes they so desperately want and can have through hypnosis.

Tom is an international instructor and in-demand Speaker, and is the award winning author of *The Book on Back Pain: The Ultimate Guide to Permanent Relief, The Change Sequence*, and Co-author of *Thinking Therapeutically: Hypnotic Skills and Strategies Explored*. Additionally, he is a Director at Contemporary College of Therapeutic Studies UK, where he trains others also wanting to embark on an enriching and fulfilling career in making a difference to others' lives, whilst also co-ordinating SelfHelpSchool™, which provides Self Help through education for the public. Tom, who is known as 'The Changeologist', consults 'leading lights' in the arenas of sport, art and music, as well as the corporate world, all who are committed to inspirational change and growth strategies using the power of the mind. You can contact Tom at Change@TomBarber.co.uk

Declutter Your Mind for Success

ERIN MULDOON STETSON

"My baggage", "your baggage", "his baggage" —phrases thrown around in casual conversation as much as an actual suitcase is thrown around by handlers at an airport. What does it mean when we talk about our "baggage?" After all, we're not actually referring to that matching set of luggage your mother bought you after college, are we? No, we are talking about the emotional and life experience "stuff" you pick up along the way; the stuff that weighs you down and makes the inside of your head hurt.

When we take a trip, our baggage literally gets heavier and messier with each souvenir we add. And, if you're like me, you can't wait to unpack and put the dirty laundry in the wash where it belongs. Similarly, in life every experience comes with emotional as well as physical stuff. Unfortunately, not all of it is as pleasurable as the mementos from vacation. Plus, when unpacking, most of us take a look at what comes out of the suitcase so we can put it where it belongs.

But, when it comes to emotional baggage, people tend to stuff it away without really looking at it. What they are doing is filling up the emotional equivalent of a classic, overstuffed closet; the one where, when you open the door, a thousand things come crashing down on your head. The one where you don't open the door except maybe a couple inches now and then to stuff more things into the dark, scary closet.

On an emotional level, that stuffing is doing you no good at all. In fact, all that clutter is not relegated to your subconscious mind. It affects all parts of your mind, as well as your body and spirit. It causes pain, disease and emotional issues. It can block you in countless ways—from achieving your potential, living authentically and manifesting abundance in your life.

Why is your mind so cluttered in the first place? It's because you've been "collecting" experiences, memories and feelings for a lifetime. Even in the womb, there may have been alarming and confusing experiences. If you had a difficult birth, or traumatic first few moments of life, the imprint of those experiences is still with you. To add insult to injury, as a baby, you may have often struggled to be understood or to have your needs met while your bumbling care givers tried to figure out if you were hungry, sleepy or needed a diaper change. How frustrating that must have been. Those early experiences went into your collection.

Think about the clutter you have collected. I suggest that, as you read this, you jot down the thoughts that pop into your head. No doubt you will start to think of your own personal clutter that is stuffed inside you somewhere. Your notes will help you when you decide to clear that clutter out. Remember, you need to look at all of it squarely before you can put it away for good.

The collection of emotional clutter goes on throughout your life. In the toddler years, you stumble and fall (literally), and struggle to communicate only to be utterly misunderstood. Then, as a teen, you stumble figuratively as you try to find your way, and still find communication difficult as your values change in relation to those of parents, teachers or even your peers.

Think about it:

- A humiliating experience in class when a teacher scolded you in front of everyone.

- Someone you had a crush on treated you with contempt.

- A vicious, behind-the-back bullying campaign waged by an alleged "friend."

- A time when you were unkind or ungrateful to someone who didn't deserve it.

- The day you walked out of a store with a pack of gum you didn't pay for.

Each of these experiences is jarring. Every single one of them can disrupt the energy system in your body and mind. It's no wonder you feel so overwhelmed with the clutter.

I vividly remember something that happened when I was 12 years old. I received a scathing note from one of my "best friends" who happened to live across the street. It was poetic in its poignancy. "Erin, you think you're hot shit on a silver platter, but really you're just cold diarrhea on a paper plate!" Wow. That hurt. It's funny now —I mean really funny — and I'm so impressed with the verbiage. But at the time, I cried big tears —the kind of tears that I thought might never stop gushing. I had to re-think my whole persona. Did I really think that I was "hot shit?" And was I actually "just cold diarrhea?" I collected the anger, the sadness and the insecurity of that moment and buried it all in my mind, heart and body.

For the record, I'm not saying that any of the experiences I'm mentioning were bad, or good, for that matter. Nor am I saying that my friend in the "hot shit" story was wrong for writing that note. What I am saying is that our experiences stay with us, in one form or another, and often create disruptions in our energy systems.

Have you been able to jot down a few notes about memories of your own that may have stayed with you and created disruptions in your own life? Job struggles, relationship or parenting challenges, heartache, loss, trauma—the little things and the big things that may be stuffed away, buried, doing some damage unbeknownst to you.

All of these things go into your collection. Don't judge them. Don't judge yourself. Simply write down a "title" for the memory. We'll address it later and possibly let go of it with ease. You won't lose the memory, but merely the negative charge that is connected to it.

Now that you have started to examine your impressive collection, you can understand how it has grown exponentially over your lifetime. You can imagine how your mind has gotten cluttered. It's no wonder so many people feel weighed down, bottled up, distracted and even confused at times.

It is possible to declutter your mind if you have the proper tools. There is a process you can use to fix the effects of that build-up.

Pat yourself on the back for beginning this journey. It's going to be fun!

TAPPING

Tapping is based on Emotional Freedom Techniques (EFT). It is a relatively new discovery that has provided thousands with relief from pain, disease and emotional issues. It can alleviate the most common matters (fear of public speaking) to the most extreme (chronic debilitating back pain), and a wide array of "stuff" in between. Basically, tapping is mind/body healing. It is a combination of ancient Chinese knowledge and modern psychology.

Tapping produces a relaxation response in your body and mind and creates an emotional contentment in the present moment. It is wonderfully simple and effective, and it is accomplished by stimulating well established energy meridian points on your body.

"How do you do that?"

You do that by tapping on particular points with your fingertips while focusing on the issue at hand. "

Really?" "It's not more complicated than that?"

Yes, really. And no, it's not more complicated than that. Plus, the process is easy to memorize, and portable—you can do it anywhere. You only need your hands and your mind.

It is my goal to make this real healing easy and accessible to you. For the entrepreneur feeling overwhelmed, or the person who has dreams of starting a business but is blocked by fear, these techniques can help create such fundamental shifts that walls tumble and doors open. The healing path of body, mind and spirit lies ahead.

So how does tapping differ, say, from other energy healing modalities such as acupuncture? By focusing on the mind-body connection, EFT tapping harnesses the power of the mind and combines it with the body's energy to propel healing to a level that could not otherwise be achieved. The techniques essentially bring a psychotherapeutic element to the energy meridians long familiar to alternative healers.

The power of thought and its effects on our well-being are no longer considered theoretical. The evidence is piling up. So let's declutter your mind so that your thoughts no longer sabotage you but can have the impact you want them to!

EFT TAPPING IN ACTION

Let's look at a particular, very real scenario that will be familiar to many. I like to call it the fear of public writing. Now, we could also address the fear of public speaking or something else but, given the fact that I overcame my fear of public writing to write this chapter, it seems an apropos example. Additionally, the fear of public writing can be a huge deal for an entrepreneur, especially when you are expected to publish a blog, post on Facebook and update your website on a regular basis.

EFT tapping has the unique ability to handle your fears and turn them into calm cool action. Whether you feel paralyzed at the thought of doing an activity like writing, or are shy about sharing what you've already written, EFT tapping can help put those fears in check.

For example, have you hesitated to write a book because of your anxiety about the fact that the dreaded written word can never be erased? It will be "out there" speaking for you, for all time. If you are like I was, that thought paralyzes you. But here I am, writing this. And enjoying it, I might add. How am I able to face my fears so courageously?

As I mentioned above, the answer is quite simple and incredibly revolutionary. I can't wait to share this fabulous secret with you. Tap along with me. You won't be sorry. Then we can high five on the other side of this silly fear that's holding you back from your greatness.

EFT IN A NUTSHELL

The body contains a network of energy points and energy channels — actual locations that can be accessed through tapping. In addition to the physical act of tapping on these specific points, EFT involves the use of words. The power of words, of language, to channel and manifest intention is hardly in question any more. So with EFT, you will use words first to acknowledge the details of the negative — the big pieces of junk cluttering your mind.

Looking at them and facing them is the first step to releasing the junk you've been shoving into your suitcase for so long. Finally, positive language is used to manifest what you want to bring into your life after you've "put away" the clutter where it belongs. Where is that? It's where your clutter can no longer hurt you.

So, let's return to our hypothetical case of a person (maybe you) who is afraid to write. This fear is getting in the way of your business, your success and your ability to create abundance in your life. Below are the simple steps that I would walk you through if you were this hypothetical person. In no time, you would be writing and publishing.

STEP 1

Close your eyes and think about what is holding you back from writing and publishing that book or updating your blog. Once you have something specific in mind, give it a number on a scale of 0-10, ten being the most intense. If you have many things running through your mind, write them down and start with the one specific issue that has the highest intensity. Think of it as the biggest piece of junk in that closet—the one that might actually knock you out if it fell on your head. Give that piece of junk a "title"—you don't need to write down the whole sordid history or explanation of the issue, just its title. The number you assign to that issue is extremely important. It allows you to compare how you feel before and after tapping.

For example, you may be thinking: "What if my ex reads this and thinks, 'what the %&*# is she writing about? Why was I ever with that chick? What a weirdo!'" Or perhaps you are thinking, "No one who reads this will ever want to talk to me, meet me or hire me. I'll be ruined."

Your title for this piece of mental debris might be: Fear of Rejection. Maybe it earns a level of 8, 9 or even 10, depending on how paralyzing it is. (You insert whichever number makes sense for how you feel in the present moment.)

STEP 2

Tap continuously with your fingers on each of the following spots while repeating the corresponding phrases out loud. (If you think a diagram might be helpful, please visit http://taponit.com.)

Karate Chop Spot (this is the place on the side of your hand you would use if you were to use a karate chop to break a piece of wood): Tap continuously with four fingers on that spot while saying the following phrase three times aloud: "Even though I am afraid of being judged and rejected [insert here: by my ex or by future clients] for what I write, I'm still a really good person."

- **Eyebrow point** (this is the beginning of your eyebrow closest to your nose): Tap continuously with two fingers at that spot and repeat the following phrase: "I'm afraid that my [ex or future client] is going to judge me and my writing in a negative way." Repeat Once.

- **Side of eye** (this is the bone bordering the outside corner of your eye): Tap continuously with two fingers on that spot and repeat the following phrase: "What if my [ex or future client] reads what I wrote and thinks I'm a terrible writer?" Repeat Once.

- **Under the eye** (about ½ inch below): Tap continuously with two fingers, saying: "I'm nervous to put myself out there. I will be laughed at." Repeat once.

- **Under the nose** (this is the philtrum: the small indentation between the bottom of your nose and the top of your upper lip): Tap continuously with two fingers on that spot while you say: "I'm afraid that someone [my ex or a judgmental future client] is going to read my writing if I put it out there." Repeat once.

- **Chin** (the spot midway between the bottom of your chin and your lower lip): Tap continuously with two fingers on that spot and say: "I'm not sure if I can handle the embarrassment of having my writing judged by [my ex, a future client] or anyone else for that matter." Repeat once.

- **Collarbone**: Tap continuously with four fingers along your collarbone towards your breast bone. Say these words: "I'm not ready to have my thoughts and ideas critiqued and ridiculed." Repeat once.

- **Under arm** (four inches below your armpit, on the side of your body): Tap continuously with four fingers: "I'm nervous that [my ex or a future client] will read what I'm writing and make fun of me." Repeat once.

- **Crown of head**: Tap continuously with all five fingers in a circular motion on the top of your head: "I'm afraid that [my ex or anyone] is going to read my writing and laugh at me." Repeat once.

- **Eyebrow point**: "I'm okay now." Repeat once.

- **Side of eye**: "I can relax now." Repeat once.

- **Under the eye**: "I am calm and relaxed." Repeat once.

- **Under the nose**: "My confidence is growing." Repeat once.

- **Chin**: "I am feeling more and more confident about my writing." Repeat once.

- **Collarbone**: "I am excited to write an awesome [book, article, blog]." Repeat once.

- **Under arm**: "I can't wait to write my [book, article, blog]." Repeat once.

- **Top of head**: "I'm ready to write and publish an amazing [book, article, blog]." Repeat once.

When you are done, take a deep breath and hold it. Then let it out in a slow, smooth exhalation.

STEP 3

After completing the tapping and repetitions, reassess the intensity of your feelings about the topic (in this case, public writing), using the scale you used originally, from 0 to 10, with ten being the strongest. Write down your response, the number and something about how you feel. Comment about whether there were any qualitative changes to the way you view or feel about the topic. If your number is still high, then repeat the process.

Be clear in acknowledging any change. For example, "After tapping, my fear of rejection and judgment regarding my writing from [my ex or future clients] is at about a level two, down significantly from my previous level of eight."

The three steps outlined above are how you use EFT to overcome your fear of public writing. You can use the same format to cope with other issues that are holding you back. The phrases that you use in your repetitions during tapping will vary according to what you are trying to release. Here are some examples:

- **Karate Chop Spot**: "Even though I'm afraid that my family will disown me because what I want to write about is too off the grid for them, I have confidence and love. I forgive them for their potential judgments." Repeat three times.

- **Karate Chop Spot**: "Even though I fear that my ideas will change one day, and what I write will be 'out there' forever, reminding me of how foolish I was, I deeply and completely love and accept myself."

- **Karate Chop Spot**: "Even though my writing isn't perfect, it's a work in progress that never seems to end. I am whole, and complete, and fabulous just as I am right now, and so is my writing."

- **Karate Chop Spot**: "Even though I feel as if I don't have time to write, I am willing to make changes in my life because I deeply and completely love and accept myself."

The intended and very real outcome of EFT tapping in this circumstance is increased self-confidence. Whether it is your writing or something else that is standing in your way, your confidence will grow exponentially the more you tap. You will laugh at your previous fears. To use our example of fearing the reaction of your ex, once you have utilized EFT tapping, you might assume that, should he read your writing, he'll wonder how he ever let someone like you get away!

Our fears about what might happen are often times more intense than any actual, potential outcome. Tapping creates equilibrium between that fear and what is real. It will allow you to gain a calm, cool perspective regarding the debris that was weighing you down by cluttering up your suitcase or your closet –in other words, your mind!

Decluttering your mind through EFT tapping applies to literally any aspect of your life. It can help you find fulfillment, success, and enjoyment in any arena: relationships, money, body image, health etc. Starting with identifying what is holding you back, seeing it for what it is and then releasing it, you ultimately replace it with something wholesome that will help you move forward.

The things that are holding you back are all that junk we talked about earlier: Fears or objections (the "I can't" mentality), obstacles — perceived or real (time, logistics) — and ultimately your "story" – the belief system that holds you where you are instead of helping you get to where you want to be.

The process that works for your mind can also be used to declutter your body. There is a holistic connection between and among mind, body and spirit, which means that detoxing one will help you declutter the others.

Your spirit can be decluttered and detoxified too. In using EFT techniques for the spirit, you will address matters of perspective, outlook and attitude. The law of attraction is essentially at work every time you succumb to fear or, conversely, feel optimistic. When you fear an outcome and fixate on that fear, you are focusing on what is essentially a belief system based on fear. Your mind, as well as your actions, reflects that belief system and you will manifest the very things you are afraid of.

When you can tap on and release the fear, you can recreate a belief system based on positive emotions, optimism and confidence. You become that person and your every action reflects those new beliefs.

So what does this mean for you? It means that EFT tapping can bring you more comfort, love and enjoyment in life. It can help you rid yourself of the heavy baggage and clutter that get in the way of being your most successful self.

To learn more about the benefits of tapping, please visit http://taponit.com.

Purpose and Living Your Passion Cure

RON BELL

T his chapter is about Ron Bell's defining your *Purpose and Living Your Passion Cure*. It offers 10 powerful ways to discover true inner peace and happiness. However, in order to understand each step in this process, we need to begin with two basic definitions.

First we'll look at the word purpose. Purpose is the reason for which something is done or created or for which something exists. Some useful synonyms are motive, motivation, cause, occasion, reason, basis, justification. When used as a verb, purpose is one's intention or objective. It has such synonyms as: intend, mean, aim, plan, design, decide, resolve, determine, propose, aspire. For example, I know someone who gets up every morning and purposefully begins to work on his goals at 6 am. He does not stop until 4 pm. He has a plan, the resolve to fulfill it and the motivation to meet all challenges. In other words, while his day is filled with purpose he also has a purpose.

Next we'll define the word passion. Passion is strong and barely a controllable emotion. The man in the previous example works, plays and rests on purpose. He is driven. The emotions he feels are strong, sometimes barely controllable; he needs to move through his days with a sense of purpose, resolve and determination. He is filled with passion.

The first question that begs to be asked, of course, is how do you get to such a place? How do you get on purpose and become motivated to stay there? One step is to begin with an inventory of your strengths. The way to do this is to ask yourself a series of questions. Ask yourself a question and the mind will always answer. Always. For example: Are you loyal? Do you pursue your assignments with pertinacity? Why do you act the way you do when faced with difficulty? Are you courageous? Honest? What are your greatest assets? Write your answers down on a piece of blank paper. Do you act on purpose throughout the day? How about passion—do you act with and feel great emotion that drives you forward toward your purpose, a passion that takes your strengths and carries them toward perfection? Create a list of the resources you, as an individual, possess and that you can get behind both mentally and emotionally.

There's wisdom in knowing your strengths: Men or women who know their strengths are never without resources. They can turn to this tool box whenever some difficulty or trouble passes through their lives. Your strengths can be the difference between staying on task (or purpose) and falling back into the rut that most people live in. This is why it's so important to combine purpose and passion. Acting on purpose from minute to minute depends completely on your motivation, and your motivation is very much about passion. The greater your emotional investment in your action, the greater will be that which drives you. Think of passion as the gas that runs the car of purpose. You can't go anywhere on an empty tank. Similarly, you can't run on gas tainted by water. You will eventually falter and stall, placing you right back where you used to be. Yes, purpose and passion go hand in hand.

Now for the *10 powerful ways to discover true inner peace and happiness:*

STEP 1: EMBRACE CHANGE

Did you know that the average person hates change? In fact, they spend their lives trying to build cocoons to keep change at bay. Little do they know that, like the butterfly, we are a chrysalis that is turned into a human version of the butterfly by the pressure of change. If, in your life, you are receiving the same results, you must change what you are doing. Then and only then will you receive a different result. Knowing this, shouldn't we learn to embrace change? Get serious about it! Determine what your natural gifts and talents are. This list will be different than the one you made regarding your strengths. This list is about the thing(s) you know, without a doubt, that you are better at than anyone else. In fact it's probably the one single and natural thing you dream about spending your life doing. (Your true Passion).

How do you begin working on using the strengths and talents you've found to create positive changes in your life? The answer is, become conscious of the choices you make on a moment-to-moment basis. Create awareness of what it is you are thinking, saying and doing throughout your day. Then begin to make these choices on purpose and with passion.

Part of making positive change in your life is identifying your dreams. Your dreams will probably rotate around those gifts or talents you discovered a few steps back. For example, somewhere within that dream vacation is also a dream of how you came to be there. What is your dream job? Why? How can you achieve it? I'll tell you how ....

Once you've clearly identified your dreams, you need to understand that turning them into reality is all about goal setting. It requires that you reverse engineer those big dreams, breaking them down until you arrive at some task you can do today and in the days to come.

Stay disciplined and focused. Once you begin setting daily goals it's very important that you stay disciplined. No weekdays off or early check-outs for you. True goal-setting requires that you spend your day focused on each goal you apply yourself to—one at a time, hour by hour and day by day—until you reach that far away dream which can create and inner peace and true happiness.

STEP 2: FIND PURPOSE AND PASSION

Self-empowerment is the actuation of the self through minute-to-minute choices. These are choices made on purpose, with real focus and passion. It's the result of knowing your strength and your dreams and having a plan, through goal-setting, to use those strengths to get there.

However, all these changes can increase your stress levels. Happily, the way to decrease stress is to take the task at the top of your prioritized list of goals and put all your focus on it, never thinking of any of the other tasks on your list until you have finished the one you are currently working on—even if you don't finish your list of daily goals. In such a case they just get added to the next day's list. Why does this work? It works because it eliminates worry (most likely one of your biggest stressors). It will also let you get more done than any other system you might happen to try.

I'll tell you a secret. The system of goal-setting I've been talking about will create a new zest for life in you, and it will leave you happier. Why? You'll have virtually eliminated worry in your life. Secondly, our minds are goal-oriented machines. By creating a focused plan, you'll be tapping into that problem-solving aspect of your mind, and it will leave you satisfied at the end of each day. A person who is satisfied with where they are in life and with whatever they have will generally be happier.

Lifestyle change, which is huge and what most individuals desire, will come as you change the decisions you make throughout the day. Make the conscious choice to make positive decisions leading to your goals. Make an extra sale a week, 50 more telephone calls per week, or take on more responsibility at work—all these changes tend to lead to lifestyle changes. So can your daily decisions: the choice to not go for a coffee break at the local café puts more money in your pocket every day; the simple choice to smile in the moment can bring all sorts of changes to your life as you meet new people and enamour the ones you know. The list is endless. Change your moment-to-moment choices and watch your life alter before your eyes.

As you become a more confident decision-maker and an even more stellar goal-setter, you'll undoubtedly notice that your personal confidence will grow exponentially. There's something about making the right choices and doing the right things (for you) that boosts people's confidence immensely.

And … you may never work again. This point may seem silly to you, but it holds a kernel of truth. When you begin to act on purpose, pursuing goals designed to bring you your greatest dreams, you'll find that you're no longer working but rather you're having fun and experiencing happiness. You'll be filled with a passion for action. No longer will problems plague you, because you'll know that each problem solved takes you a step closer to the fulfilment of your daily goals and your ultimate dreams.

STEP 3: SEVERAL INTERTWINED METHODS FOR OBTAINING INNER PEACE

One way to obtain inner peace is to go in deep with meditation. There are many different forms of meditation, and it's beyond the scope of this piece to point you in a specific direction. Suffice it to say that meditation serves two purposes: 1) to clear the mind and 2) to create an intense feeling of focus and well-being. By going deep into a meditative state you can face whatever it is that lies before you with a renewed sense of passion and clarity of thought. Sounds good doesn't it?

Joining up and networking with individuals who are on a "passion" quest for the gift or talent that will light a fire beneath them like never before is heady stuff and very important. You must surround yourself with "like" minded individuals. These are people who are excited by the prospect of finally discovering and doing what they were born to do. They're a special club of people who are passionately working on achieving their dreams. And that excitement will rub off on you. I am personally involved with a Success Training Company called PEAK POTENTIALS. If you would personally like to take your life to the next level, I recommend you attend their self-development seminar. It's a true life-changing event. You may register at: http://lifepurposeandpassionbook.com/ -- a great group of people to rub shoulders with! You've got to know this will lead to greater inner peace.

Fasting is a biblical way to truly humble yourself in the sight of God (Psalm 35:13; Ezra 8:21). King David said, "I humble myself through fasting."

Fasting can transform your prayer life into a richer and more personal experience. Fasting can also result in a dynamic personal revival in your own life and can make you a channel of revival to others.[1] It most definitely leads to inner peace.

And finally, self-reflection, like fasting, can clear your mind. Serious thought about one's character, actions, and motives can bring a sense of cohesiveness that can't help but create a greater sense of peace.

STEP 4: DISCOVER YOUR LIFE PURPOSE

Many people never discover their "life purpose." They get caught up in earning a living, raising a family and a thousand other different things. They might play wistfully with a hobby they love or they might daydream about doing something they secretly think would bring them the true contentment they desire. But they never quite reach the point where they make the jump to living their dreams.

The truth of the matter is that *Success is ... taking action.* One must become actively aware of what it is that they were put on this earth to do. You know what this is. It's that secret dream you hardly dare to dream of. Or it's something people have always said you were born to do. Whatever your gift or talent is, deep down you know it. You just need to bring it to the forefront of your mind, you need to seek true awareness. Next comes action. The average person never takes enough small steps to create the momentum needed to move forward into the life of their dreams. Success is ... taking action. Break your dreams down into ever smaller tasks until you reach the point where you have a list of things you can do now—today. Act on them. Take the thousand baby steps that will add up to massive action. Begin right now. The number of people who begin the journey to their dreams but never get there are countless. It's not their fault. They never knew that they had to carefully analyze their actions. A ship gets to its destination by making the minute-to-minute analysis of its position and then making course adjustments necessary to stay moving in the direction of the targeted port of call. Do not try to "eat" the whole elephant. Focus and take small steps to reach the bigger goal. Take realistic steps to reach your goals and obtain your dreams because, when you make unrealistic goals, you set yourself up for frustration and ultimately failure. People must chase their dreams in the same way. We must constantly adjust what we do to make sure we stay on the right path.

You might think this path will be too stressful. And stress can kill. Everyone knows that. Well, if you don't want stress then you must first accept that happiness, joy, contentment and beauty are the natural order of things. Did you know that 47% of all cancer cases is due to "pent up anger and resentment? Strive for continued happiness. It may be a stretch at first, because I can almost guarantee you don't have these things in your daily life. It's not your fault. Chances are no one ever taught you how to consciously focus on bringing them into your daily life. That's right: the key to removing stress from your life is to purposely bring happiness, joy, contentment and beauty into your life by making the right choices on a minute-to-minute basis. It's that simple and that difficult. But you can do it. I know you can.

You really must choose the environments mentioned above. Toxic environments kill everything in their path. You must choose to live differently, every minute of your life. And you can't expect to be valued if you don't, first, value yourself. Change your thinking and your actions will change, and people will sense it. They will look at you differently. Because we are, most definitely what we think. The Process of Manifestation is: Thoughts lead to Feelings. Feelings lead to Actions. Actions lead to Results. Let's get Positive RESULTS in our lives!! Your inner thoughts will determine your outer world!

STEP 5: LEARN TO THINK POSITIVELY

Many people think that positive thinking implies seeing the world through rose-colored lenses, and ignoring or glossing over the negative aspects of life. You know—the glass is half full instead of half empty. However, positive thinking actually means approaching life's challenges with a positive outlook. It does not necessarily mean avoiding or ignoring the bad things; instead, it involves making the most of potentially bad situations, trying to see the best in other people, and viewing yourself and your abilities in a positive light. Such habits reduce stress and increase your level of contentment and happiness.

Why is positive thinking contagious? This is what I call a "no brainer." Who would you rather hang out with: the guy who is always the life of the party or the grumpy guy in the next cubicle at work? The choice is obvious, right? But why is it obvious? It's obvious because the guy who's the life of the party makes you feel good—about the party and about yourself. And therein lies the key. If you alter how you view yourself and your abilities, other people will alter their behaviours regarding you. Call it the psychology of the masses or some other technical term: it doesn't change the fact that, in general, people respond to us based on how we see ourselves.

How can you turn negative thinking into positive thinking? Positive thinking must be made a habit for it to work. That means you must be willing to consciously choose your thoughts or your response to what is going on in your life from a minute-to-minute standpoint, until the process becomes second nature. This takes commitment and hard work, something most people aren't going to do for a process they don't even understand. But you now understand, don't you?

An example of positive thinking: "The history of the baby frog.......

Once upon a time there was a bunch of baby frogs....
… participating in a competition. The target was to get to the top of a high tower. A crowd of people had gathered to observe the race and encourage the participants.....

The start shot rang out.......
Quite honestly:
None of the onlookers believed that the baby frogs could actually accomplish getting to the top of the tower.
They said things like:"Åh, it's too difficult!!!
They'll never reach the top."
or: "Not a chance... the tower is too high!"
One by one some of the baby frogs fell off…
...Except those who quickly climbed higher and higher..
The crowd kept on yelling:
"It's too difficult. Nobody is going to make it!"More baby frogs became tired and gave up...
...But one kept going higher and higher.....
He was not giving up!

At the end everybody had given up, except the one determined to reach the top! All the other participants naturally wanted to know how he had managed to do what none of the others had been able to do!

One competitor asked the winner, what was his secret?

The truth was.......

The winner was deaf!!!!

The lesson to be learned:

Don't ever listen to people who are negative and pessimistic...

...they will deprive you of your loveliest dreams and wishes you carry in your heart! Always be aware of the power of words, as everything you hear and read will interfere with your actions!

Therefore:

Always stay...

POSITIVE!

And most of all:

Turn a deaf ear when people tell you that you cannot achieve your dreams!

Always believe:

You can make it! Stay Positive!!!

STEP 6: ELIMINATE NEGATIVITY

Until you've become strong enough to be able to ward off the negativity in situations it would be a great idea to avoid watching the news. It might even be good to avoid television altogether. Why? Because there's so much that is negative or that will counter your attempts to live a contented and happy lifestyle that it could severely hamper your efforts.

Just to make a point. I turned on the television last night when I got home, and set about having a relaxing evening. There were at least six channels that were talking about current terrorism threats and many other channels were carrying shows full of violence and bloodshed. Tell me how that works to help you change your mindset in a positive way? I'm not saying not to watch television, but be very careful what you put into your psyche.

What was said previously goes double for negative environments. If a situation truly is negative, how do you expect to truthfully change your thoughts about it? You can do it, but you'll most likely be kidding yourself. The way to stay positive, contented and happy is to make certain your day is filled with light and beauty, not darkness and ugliness. Make sense?

Adopt healthy eating habits. Is thinking about having a hamburger and French fries for lunch really bad thinking? It is if you're overweight and your goal is to lose that weight. To adopt healthy eating habits (and this goes for anyone, not just the overweight), one must make those moment-to-moment positive choices we've been talking about. The choice to choose a salad over a hamburger and fries is simple—if you are acting on "purpose."

Focus on the "whats" not the "what ifs." What can I do about my current situation to make it a positive and joyful experience? What if this wasn't happening to me? What if I just skipped out? What if I made the effort to enjoy myself? Which of these questions will make certain my thoughts and actions are going to ensure the best possible experience? If you chose question the first one, then you're beginning to get the hang of "positive thinking." Do not look at opportunities and situations in life and say, "I'll believe it when I see it". You will miss opportunities over and over again. It's the exact opposite, YOU WILL SEE IT WHEN YOU BELIEVE IT" Have Faith! Just because you do not see the seeds growing, doesn't mean, they are not growing. Please refer to the story of the Chinese Bamboo Tree—the story of patience.

What do you love? What do you love to do? I'm not just talking about work here. What leisure activities do you love? What can you do to make sure you build as many of these activities into your days as possible? Remember the goal-setting process? By placing leisure activities on your priority list, you'll be sure to do them when their turn arrives. If I've booked a tee time at my favourite golf course for 2 pm, then I know my workday is going to end at two, and I can prioritize my daily to-do list accordingly, knowing that no matter what happens I will quit working at that time.

Will such practices work every time? Of course not. Life is full of problems and obstacles. But I can guarantee that such habits will bring more pleasure and inner peace into your life than any other method I know of.

STEP 7: DEVELOP YOUR "SELF"

The threat to your continued self-development is inaction. Regardless of the reason or excuse, you can't change anything about your life unless you take purposeful, massive action. Those countless moment-to-moment choices that lead to action of unimaginable proportions must be made on purpose and with specific results in mind. Failure to do this consistently is the one major threat to the achievement of anything you want—include self-development. Best Selling Author T. Harv Eker was quoted saying, "Rich Minded People continue to learn and Grow and Poor "minded" and Middle Class people think that they already know." It's key to invest in your continuous self-development.

Find a life coach. Why do you need a life coach? A person who has already done the things you want to do can guide you past the many pitfalls that lie before you. She can also ensure that you make the right moment-to-moment decisions. She's been there, remember? A successful life coach can shorten your journey by years. Isn't that worth the investment of money and effort? I think it is.

Associate with like minds. People have the ability to affect others through changes in their mindset and their actions. Imagine what could happen if like-minded people came together. The effect could be explosive. I know for a fact that two like-minded people can increase their success exponentially. It's like they form a third mind, a "mastermind," that lifts them up and carries them forward. The effect increases as you add more people to your group. You can even have more than one mastermind group. Some will focus on personal development, some on work and some on investing. You can have a mastermind group for just about any aspect of your life. Anytime two or more like-minded people get together great things can happen.

Read self-help books. Again, you can benefit from those who have gone before you. There are thousands of self-help books out there. And they cover just about any subject you can imagine. Invest in them. There isn't any rule that says your mentor must be a live person. Books can and do teach people how to attain their goals in life.

Enrol in self-development programs. Dale Carnegie, perhaps the greatest motivator ever, taught many, many thousands of people how to achieve their dreams. His books touched many others. His speaking courses were genius in motion. Enrolling in similar courses can give each of us the spark to move forward, to take action with a purpose. You don't have to do this thing alone. Find a program to help you along.

Everything that has been laid down in this outline could be considered the process by which you can change your character and/or your abilities for the better. Don't you think that such positive changes would make you happier and more at peace with yourself? All that remains is for you to take action.

STEP 8: LEARN THE LAW OF ATTRACTION

The law of attraction is the name given to the term that "like attracts like" and that by focusing on positive or negative thoughts, one can bring about positive or negative results. This belief is based upon the idea that people and their thoughts are both made from "pure energy" and the belief that like energy attracts like energy. One example used by a proponent of the law of attraction is that if a person opened an envelope expecting to see a bill, then the law of attraction would "confirm" those thoughts and contain a bill when opened. A person who decided to instead expect a cheque might, under the same law, find a cheque instead of a bill. Although there are some cases where positive or negative attitudes can produce corresponding results, there is no scientific basis to the law of attraction.

How to use the Law of Attraction and how it may assist you: "The one who speaks most about illness has illness. The one who speaks about prosperity has prosperity," Esther and Jerry Hicks write. "You attract all of it." By focusing on something, you make it happen. And oh how true this is. In life focus can be everything. Think about something long enough and hard enough and you're sure to become attuned to actions that can make it happen. The intense focus will also increase the chances that you will act on your thoughts when the opportunity presents itself.

It's very easy for people who know this secret to believe that like attracts like, but I caution against that belief. What is actually happening is you are becoming more alert to and more ready to take the actions that will lead to whatever it is you want. Make enough such choices and you are almost certain to arrive at your destination. And it can really feel like magic!

Successful people know many of the things I've been writing about. They know that if they put themselves out there they will eventually bump into something like they are looking for, whether that's a person, a place, or a thing. It's all about focus and the choices that result.

The old adages are that we reap what we sow, that what goes around comes around and that what we give so shall we receive. The whole point is that our focus/choice combination works every way. Put your focus on giving something different to your community or to your family and you will tend to make choices that will reflect that change in thinking. The changes will be noticed by others, who you can be certain will eventually return the favour however they can. It's a great way to live and you can reap rewards beyond your imagination.

STEP 9: TAKE YOUR QUALITY OF LIFE TO THE NEXT LEVEL

There is nothing so strong and so life-affirming as love. Felice Leonardo "Leo" Buscaglia PhD (March 31, 1924 – June 12, 1998), also known as "Dr. Love," was an American author and motivational speaker, and a professor in the Department of Special Education at the University of Southern California. He believed that, the more you love, the greater becomes your capacity for love, a rather contrary vision of what love is like. This was a view of love as having the infinite power to change us and those around us. In fact he said as much in the following quote: *Too often we underestimate the power of a touch, a smile, a kind word, a listening ear, an honest compliment, or the smallest act of caring, all of which have the potential to turn life around.* – Leo Buscaglia

I could go a step further and say that the greatest phenomenon in the universe is the concept of love. Many see God as love. A fact I know is that the more you give love, the more you tend to receive, whether you're thinking of God or yourself or another. Yes, self-love is important. We can only love our God or our spouse or anyone else as much as we love ourselves. How can it be any different? We can only give what we have and what we know.

This also goes for the intensity of our love. It is our deep belief and our intensity that gives us the power to affect others. For this reason it is a worthwhile exercise to practice intensity of love.

I also admonish you to give as you hope to receive. We have all heard this platitude. It has lost what power it might ever have had. But this does not diminish the truth. If you are willing to sacrifice to give to another or to your community, then you fundamentally change yourself. You become more willing to help, to put yourself out there. People will remember this. So, when the time comes when you are in need, as we all are at some point in life, you'll find that all your sacrifices will be remembered and returned tenfold. It may not be in the way you expect, but it will happen. There's too much anecdotal evidence to believe otherwise.

And as I close, love once again comes into play. Open your heart to the universe and it will fill you up. Give all this back and you will feel as you have never felt before. Some call it a religious conversion, others refer to it as enlightenment; still others speak of a sense of peace and happiness. The bottom line is that you can't love too much. It's impossible. Love can't be used up, so don't be afraid to reach out (take action) for what is waiting for you. You won't regret it.

STEP 10: MORE WAYS TO FIND TRUE INNER PEACE

Apologize and Forgive – When a person apologizes for a wrong he's done or forgives a wrong done unto her an amazing thing happens. All the negative thoughts and emotions you were harbouring simply melt away. You may want to know why this is the case. The answer is incredibly simple: you change your focus. Your moment-to-moment thoughts and actions turn away from what was bothering you and suddenly things are new again.

Relax – Inner peace is a state created by you. Taking time out of your busy day to just relax and allow your mind to drift away to your favourite destinations is a good place to start.

Be Grateful – Happiness and contentment come from being grateful for what you already have. Take your focus and place it on thoughts and actions that indicate to you that you are, indeed, grateful.

Go outdoors – Nature is the great healing balm. A walk in the forest, a stroll through your garden, a ride on your bike or any other outside activity that gets your body moving and breathing in fresh air can't help but improve your disposition.

Go Inside Yourself – The best way I know to go inside myself is meditation, which is the practicing of certain techniques that allow you to clear your mind, heighten your focus and then point your mind in the direction you wish to go.

Know When to Stand Firm – Inner peace is sometimes reached by facing down a problem, whether that be an intense short-term task or a longer-term worry. Face down your problems, find the best way to deal with them, do those things and then forget about them. Inner peace will be yours.

Learn the Power of Surrender – When people talk about surrendering they're usually talking about God. There's something amazingly powerful about giving up yourself and your problems to the holy spirit. I think the largest part of this is that you are giving up all your worries. Joe Tye (CEO and Head Coach of Values Coach Inc., which provides consulting, training and coaching on values-based life and leadership skills.) once said "Worry is ingratitude to God in advance." Think about that for a moment!

Be the Love You Want to Feel – If you want to feel loved, then you must not only love yourself but demonstrate your love for others. It's a risky thing to do—putting yourself out there like that—but you already know that we reap what we sow.

Be of Service – Strange things (good things) happen when you give of yourself to your community, the first of these being a sense of belonging, which goes a long way to creating inner peace.

Be Here Now – And, finally, making the choice to be in the moment, to enjoy each and every one we have during our time on earth, creates such a sense of joy that one soon relaxes and finds a sense of inner peace. Try it, you'll see.[2]

[2]http://www.thebridgemaker.com/10-paths-to-true-happiness/

Honor Your Inner Treasures

CELINA TIO

COLLECTIVE CREATED ME

"We are all created from our experiences, and the first step towards embracing our inner treasures is to acknowledge this. You are wonderful, and the experiences that took you to this point are all part of that. Do not be afraid of yourself; instead, let yourself shine." This quote is from my recent book, *Honor Your Inner Treasures*. It's an underlying principle of that work, and its message is most certainly applicable to what you're about to read in this chapter of *The Authorities*. Collective Created Me explains in the *Honor Your Inner Treasures* book, how most of our beliefs are obtained through training and repetition, and assumed personality through education. Becoming aware of the Collective Created Me is extremely beneficial because it puts you on the road to self-acceptance and realization, forgiveness, independence, appreciation and true happiness.

Think about this for a moment: do you remember someone in your family being sick when you were a child? Were the hours spent in family time talking about symptoms, where pain started, where it ended, how long it lasted, and medicines? It's likely that much of the conversation also revolved around nurses, doctors' assessments and trips to the hospital. Soon, with so much health and sickness related information taken in, you unconsciously started to become so familiar enough with that illness that you accepted it as just part of your family. It became so normal that you could quickly respond to questions about it as if it were your illness, too. "My uncle Charlie had it, and so did his son and my grandmother. It runs in our family."

Imagine if the conversation you heard about Uncle Charlie's illness had been about the way that healthy habits, physical activities, and letting go of toxic thoughts helped him recover. What would you have learned to do then in the event of an illness?

This example of negativity changing your perspective is applicable to other life experiences. What about love and relationships? Conversations about unfaithfulness, divorce, unhealthy relationships, abuse, violence? How has the negativity of those conversations affected your beliefs and the actions you've taken in life? Money is another example. People often say they never have enough money. Stories are shared about someone's new business failing, or friends who've lost their homes because they couldn't make their mortgage payments. Wouldn't stories of success have a more positive impact to encourage others to improve in their lives?

Most people receive diagnoses during their lives pertaining to health, personal finances, the country's economy, beauty, fashion and relationships. Usually, these diagnoses are fully accepted as truth and fact. There is an alternative, however. Why not see a diagnosis as feedback of that exact, precise moment and utilize it as the moment of opportunity to change, to create, to expand, to become, to discover, is opening up for you?

People often say when a door closes a window opens, and wait for the window to open right in front of them. Often, hoping that the window will magically pop open and the situation will change. The sad thing is, it may take a while and in the meantime the beliefs that life is not fair, life is hard or life is good to others start to run your thoughts.

I want you to know that all windows and doors are always open for you. Even more, there are no windows, there are no doors, because once you embrace your greatness you are free to live with purpose.

Going back to our example of listening to other people's life experiences, can you perceive how your fears and beliefs originated during these events? The occasions are wonderful moments to enjoy and remember the past, but sometimes people retell stories about illnesses with as much detail as they can recall. It's possible the now-adult children have no recollection of the event's seriousness because they remember with a child's naïveté only how happy they were about recovery. Now, listening to the story of an experience in your life that evoked sadness, these adults inevitably feel pulled down and relive that low-energy feeling. You can change that feeling in you and all the people around you. Next time you are at a reunion be sure to evoke moments that bring joy and laughter. Everyone will leave feeling great, having enjoyed the party, and with a more positive attitude for the next adventure in their life.

BECOME AWARE - CONNECT WITH YOUR INNER BEING

Let go of the stories and let go of others' experiences. Start living your own.

Embrace the belief that your life is complete and absolute just as is. Take a deep breath, aware of your body, starting at the top and working your way down. Begin with your scalp, your hair, your temples, your forehead, your eyebrows, your eyes, then move on until you reach the tip of your toes. It's important to take in every part of yourself so don't stop at the surface. Recognize your organs and their functions, even noting your breath as it travels into your lungs and fills you with pure oxygen. Become aware of your being. I ask that you become aware of your being, not that you look into the mirror or take a selfie and analyze it to see if you have wrinkles, or criticize your body shape. Stop judging yourself and start knowing yourself.

Selfies have become, to many, a tool to prove oneself, or a tool of confirmation of existence, presence and self-acceptance, and others' approval of the moment that is being lived.

As if the moment being lived needs external approval to be considered as a "perfect moment" and only then sharing it with the world.

When you look at the moment you are living as an image that "looks good" or "like happiness", the gap between what you are doing "looks great", and truly feeling great, is large. There is no enjoyment or happiness if it always depends on others' opinions. Making a picture look good when the emotions you are feeling at the moment don't match the illusion of the created image is keeping you from living a true honest happy moment.

Different from this is taking a picture to capture a moment of real pleasure and happiness, and the peace and joy that healthy relationships and celebrations bring. Those are photographs that recall true emotions of happiness, in turn aligning your whole being into feeling truly amazing. These selfies are not only a moment taken with a camera; they are taken into your soul, leaving a long-lasting impression in your life. Those are moments that you will truly love to share with others without deleting anything. What is your selfie telling you when you look at it? What is that image revealing?

Become aware of yourself and the moment without editing. Be completely honest about everything. In this moment of self-awareness, accept everything – your age, aches, sadness, longings, best memories, dreams – without shyness, even if they look too big at this moment. Become aware because for the first time in your life you will be truly, honestly and entirely present with yourself, as you know yourself to be at this moment. What is your inner self telling you? This is the true SELF you should be contemplating.

If you do this, for the first time in your life you will be truly, honestly and entirely present. Your unique, true self will be revealed. For many people, doing this will be the scariest meeting of their lives. To me it is the most amazing!

When working with my clients, this point of their journey is the most exciting to me. As their guide to reaching their true inner being throughout the Honor Your Inner Treasures™ Program, the transformation the client undergoes is magical, because their life suddenly expands as they embrace and accept fully their inner self.

YOUR EMOTIONS ARE POWERFUL. LEARN FROM THEM.

Pretending is the only sure thing someone does when they are denied their true feelings. Pretending to feel well, smiling just with the movement of the facial muscles, repeating clichés as a consolation to true feelings, and distancing ourselves from loved ones or hiding from life aren't effective measures. Not talking about problems doesn't solve them. On the contrary, the repetition of those actions and inner messages undoubtedly becomes the reality in your life, which extends the sadness, insecurity, lack of confidence, and low-energy life. It's an unhealthy cycle, difficult to break. Have you ever heard people complaining about the good luck of others, or blaming the sad circumstances in their life on other people's lives? If you come close to a person behaving this way, stay away. You don't want to adopt that attitude.

You can change, you can become more, and you can be the best amazing you because you truly, genuinely feel it. Sharing your life with others with honesty, because there is absolutely nothing to hide, is liberating. Accept that you are a human being experiencing life, and in the process are growing, becoming, expanding, and evolving.

Through this process there will be moments that call for change, whether of habits, beliefs, actions, or behaviors. Change is a process of evolving into a different state. The emotions that you carry through the transition are of most importance. Are you making the change out of resentment or fear? Is it happening because you don't feel you're enough? Or are you just resigning yourself because you are obedient to unhappiness. What if you make the change because you know that you would love and enjoy doing something different?

Ask yourself what you need to make this change? Maybe it's taking a course or learning something new. Going through training is a fun ride when all you are doing is acquiring new skills to master what you love to do! Don't let the fear of change keep you from becoming healthier and happier. You look and feel healthy and beautiful when you are enjoying the moments that you are creating in your life. Change gives you jolts of energy that propels you to do more.

CHANGE TO THE POSITIVE SIDE OF LIFE

"Change the thinking positive and acting negative attitude." – Celina Tio

I hear people talking about difficult situations in their lives that end with usual comments like "I'm staying positive," "I'm trying to think positive" or "Hopefully…" However, simply repeating the mantra "I'm staying positive" does not make it true. When you are vibrating in the true sense of positive energy your life has no room for negative energy. Positive will always see, hear, understand, interpret, and plan in a constructive manner. When clients come for their first consultations with me, I listen attentively to their voices. From their tones I can hear the negative energy of unhealed wounds, regardless of the words they use. They tell their stories as if they've become comfortable hurting. This is a common means of self-defense and emotional survival.

In their journeys through the Honor Your Inner Treasures™ Program, clients delve into their true selves and are guided through the process of transmuting their thoughts into a positive perspective. This transformation occurs once we do the necessary inner work at the soul level, which is the purest essence of being. Anger may become understanding and compassion; resentment an opportunity for self-reflection and inner growth; and solitude a time of self-forgiveness and self-acceptance. The more you discover about your inner being, the closer you are to the positive energy of your true self. Knowing that each step my clients take brings them closer to their inner being of positive creation gives me great joy. It is important to create life experiences in such a way that, when you reflect on the past, all you see is a magical garden of your own design that you can be proud of having imagined, lived, grown and created.

Let's do an exercise that will assist you with looking at decisions based on fear. You will need to sit comfortably on a chair and have with you a pad of paper and a pen. Imagine an "X" mark on the floor to your right that represents the change that you want to make, and an "X" to your left side. The "X" mark on the left side represents the negative reasons that you have to make the change in your life and the "X" on the right side represents positive ones.

On the paper write the reasons you want to make the change. For example, let's say that the decision you want to make is about a change in career. Write on the paper the thoughts that have crossed your mind. Use one piece of paper per thought about the issue. (It is important to follow these steps carefully.) Now, decide if the thought you've written is negative or positive and put the paper to your left or right side. Use the guide on the next page to help you determine whether your thoughts are positive or negative.

THOUGHT	LEFT SIDE	RIGHT SIDE
<u>I'm so fed up with my job.</u> I think I'll look for another one.	X	
<u>My job is so boring.</u> After doing the same thing every day for so long, it is not *exciting* anymore.	X	
I have been thinking of working part-time so I can go back to school. I'll have to cut down on expenses but I know it will be ok because I have some savings.		X
I have a job offer in another company <u>but</u> I would have to take a few courses to meet their requirement. a) I don't have the money to pay for the training b) It's hard to go back to class c) All your other "BUTS"	X	
<u>I hate going to work. The place is so toxic. The gossiping and competition is just sickening.</u>	X	

As you can see, on the column for thoughts I have underlined the negative comments. On the fourth example the word but is underlined because the "buts" are so big in our lives. You truly have to listen closely when you speak. Until you change your internal dialogue and are able to do this spontaneously, it is best to do this exercise by writing it on pieces of paper. Doing this will change the thinking positive and acting negative attitude that most people have without realizing why their lives are so difficult. Once you have identified your thought process about the issue, you can transform it and move all your thoughts to the positive side.

THOUGHT	LEFT SIDE	TRANSFORM & MOVE TO THE RIGHT SIDE
I'm so fed up with my job. I think I'll look for another one.	X	I'm more than ready to expand my possibilities. I know I have learned enough in my current position so I now realize I have room to grow.
My job is so boring. After doing the same thing every day for so long, it is not *exciting* anymore.	X	I love the feeling of excitement that bring new possibilities and learning new things. Change is great because I'm now ready.
I have been thinking of working part-time so I can go back to school. I'll have to cut down on expenses and [but] I know it will be ok because I have some savings.		This example shows how something that could be big "but I don't have money" is removed as an inconvenience and seen as something to work through.
I have a job offer in another company but I would have to take a few courses to meet their requirement. a) I don't have the money to pay for the training b) It's hard to go back to class c) All your other "BUTS"	X	This example is the opposite of the one above. Listen to all of your buts because they only pave the road ahead with more of the same in your life today. "No money" only brings you no money.
I hate going to work. The place is so toxic. The gossiping and competition is just sickening.	X	I have changed. I notice that my environment doesn't match the person that I am today. So it is time to move into a welcoming, healthy, prosperous, happy environment for me.

When you finish transforming your thought process, written now with only positive reasons, you will feel much more enthusiastic and energized to move forward and take the necessary steps to become or do. Every step of the way becomes more pleasurable because you have created a happy and positive future for yourself. What seemed to be big obstacles in the road are now the building stones and success is within reach! Congratulations! You truly do have the inner power to transform your life.

I have created a transformational workbook for my clients that enter the Honor Your Inner Treasures™ Program and as we go through the process they do simple, fun and motivating change processes. When they finish, only then the realization comes regarding how powerful it is to invest time into loving ourselves.

BELIEFS

All people have beliefs that help structure their lives. We know with great certainty that whatever we believe is true, and one of these beliefs is self-worth. People even determine their income based on their belief of self-worth. Your resume indicates exactly how much money you will make in the next year. When you review it and no changes have been made, you are hoping that inflation or the economy of the company you work for will determine the increase in the salary that you will be earning. Have you ever stopped to think about it? You are giving your power to another person to determine your growth, not only in your economy, but also your personal potential to do more, to become who you want to be.

I have worked with clients who are business owners feeling stressed out because of low funds, poor self-esteem and a lack of confidence. These issues not only impact their personal lives but also how their business grows. Those negative beliefs, ideas and limitations also have an impact on their earnings and the status of their finances, and all the people working for their company.

I remember working with Priti, a 43-year-old married woman. She emigrated to Canada from India, where she had received her degree as a software engineer. Once in Canada, Priti was able to obtain a position where she could use some of her education and experience. The reason I say 'some' of her education and experience is because when she came to see me for the first time she said that she was starting to feel bored with her job and not living up to her full potential. Priti felt that there were problems in the company that took too long to solve and required great work to make operations run more efficiently. Doing things the way the company had done for years was causing the same problems over and over again. She wanted to make a change and had a vision to do so.

However, Priti was quiet and didn't like to be the center of attention, so she kept to herself, trying to fit into the company's mold. Eventually, the conflict between shyness and wanting to change operations caused her a great deal of stress. She could not feel confident putting forth her suggestions. And although there was nothing I could do to help her with her software issues, I was able to help her build her confidence to act, speak, think and move forward. With those new positive traits, she was able to increase her self-esteem and recognize her own value.

Being foreign and fearing she might appear ignorant to others was one of Priti's greatest stumbling blocks. To offset this, I offered a metaphor. I asked her to consider the plastic casing that envelops the computer containing the software she created. Is that foreign? Obviously, the answer is no. The casing is just another part of the whole computer just as she, too, is part of the whole.

In creation nothing is foreign. We are all co-creating contributing our energy into the amazing universe we all live in. This is why it is so important that you truly live your lives from your inner treasures because underneath your fears and doubts you are pure potential, everyone has amazing positive energy to add to the whole.

We also worked on Priti's self-esteem and confidence by training her subconscious mind to act, feel and think the way the leader she desired to be would. The leader she wanted to be was one who confidently and clearly communicated her views, ideas and solutions with the tone of a manager. In just a few weeks Priti noticed she was expressing her ideas, asking questions and sharing her knowledge and experience without feeling timid. Most importantly, she noticed that her peers welcomed her ideas.

Eventually, Priti realized this company didn't have potential to grow and she was putting all of her potential in a box too small for her. She knew she was ready to move on with confidence.

That spark of inner realization of your personal self, and of how truly valuable your contribution is to everything you do, changes everything. You become confident to plan and live your life making decisions that feel right, and feel an inner peace because you gained control. Now, you have the power to do the things that are truly important to you. Once you learn to expand your consciousness beyond your fear, the limitation you had becomes limit-less.

In my upcoming book, *Limitless Beliefs - 7 Steps to Transcend into a Joyful and Abundant You*, you will find the how-to for this process. To purchase, learn more about the book, www.limitlessbeliefs.com or www.celinatioauthor.com.

YOUR LIFE IS YOUR DECISION AND YOUR CREATION

"Create your life experiences in such a way that the day you look back all you see is a magical garden of your own design that you can be proud of having imagined, lived, grown and created." – Celina Tio

"Really? Are you sure? Because I was told…" These are all comments based on a lack of confidence. This does not have to be you! You are able to declare your independence, power and freedom! To embrace the true and pure intention of creation!

I'll share with you the experience of Laura, a beautiful and intelligent woman who came to my office for help. As she introduced herself and explained the reason why she had made the appointment, I was amazed. At 32 years old, she was a successful fashion designer. Her passion, however, was singing and songwriting. What an amazing girl, and what a disparity in her professional career compared to her dreams.

Her narrative was sad due to many of her life's circumstances and events. Her self-esteem and confidence was at an all-time low after ending a relationship that was going nowhere. Now, she hoped to let go of all her little self. Laura wanted to have more confidence to make decisions and communicate her ideas and feelings, and she wanted to feel good about herself. Simply put, she wanted to live happily.

I could have told her how beautiful, amazing and intelligent I thought she was. I could have pointed out all the wonderful opportunities she could have in life or how much I admired her. But she wasn't there for me to tell her what most any friend would. She needed to know from her own heart, discovering and loving herself so that she could go through her life's journey knowing her essence.

At the end of her journey I asked Laura to write what she decided was most valuable about herself. She took a few days and sent me an e-mail describing her value as she perceived it. Imagine the courage it took to be so vulnerable. Without relying on anyone else's opinions, she confessed her own beauty, strength, warmth and intelligence. She had honored her inner treasures.

I have asked her permission to share this with you because I want you to know that it is also possible for you. She kindly and happily agreed because she felt she could help other people. Maybe that person today is you or someone you love.

"I value myself because I am a strong person who perseveres through hardship, and I have faith I will get through it. I value myself because I am loving and kind-hearted person. I value myself because I take care of those in need and treat them just as I would treat myself. I value myself because I am a hard worker and very motivated. I value myself because I am a good woman. I value myself because I have self-respect and integrity, and will not allow anyone to take that away. I value myself because I am humble in life. I value myself because I am a good sister, friend, daughter, and lover because I care for people's feelings. I value myself because of my relationship with God and how I want to continue to help myself be better. I value myself because I am a loving woman who shares love with everyone. I value myself because I can make people laugh and really bring out the best in them; this shows me how amazing I am. I value myself because even if I am scared or fearful I have courage to face those fears. I value myself because of my ability to forgive and make amends even when people have truly hurt me. I value my positive thinking and my ability to turn what can be a bad situation into a great one. I value myself because I am able to express my feelings and my emotions now in a calm and mature way. I value myself because any goal I set for myself I achieve, because I am willing to work hard. I value myself because I always keep on smiling even when the going gets tough. I value myself because I am beautiful, strong, smart, mature, funny, loving, and kind person."

- Laura, Toronto, Canada
Fashion Designer/ Singer and Songwriter, naturally from the heart.

APPRECIATION

If life were a coin, would you say it is less valuable when you are looking on the head side just because the imprinted value is on the other side and you can't see it?

The value of everything is found through deep appreciation. Lots of people walk through life with the expectation of being accepted and liked by others, but they suffer a great deal when the world around them doesn't show them what they expect. Start increasing your self-value by appreciating your life as it is in this moment. Even if your world looks or feels different than you'd like, there is value to be found. You can increase that value by describing it and saying thank you. At first, it might take some creativity if you have been depreciating things most of your life.

Let's think of something you do every day, like eating. All of us eat when we are hungry, but some also eat when anxious, nervous or depressed. There is even a name for this: comfort food. Comfort food is supposed to make you feel better when you eat it; however, nobody has ever said, "I was feeling sad and I ate a whole bowl of ice cream and now everything is fine! All of a sudden I feel loved and my finances have improved drastically with every spoonful of food I ate!" This would simply not be true.

On the other hand, when you eat because you feel hungry your body and mind feel better because they receive the nourishment needed. If you offer and share your meal and spend time in the company of family or friends, your soul is nourished as well. In preparing your meal, be grateful that you have the ingredients on hand needed to prepare the meal that will nourish every cell in your body. Imagine all the minerals, vitamins, proteins, carbohydrates and fibers that are present in what you are about to consume, and how you are benefiting from them. Thank the supermarket for having them available for you, and the people who've dedicated their life into growing them. Even thank the work you do that earns you the funds to buy your food. It's crucial to become aware of the dimension of what you are about to eat.

- Be grateful to the soil that has the perfect nutrients to grow your food.

- Be grateful to the sun and the water for adding their energy.

- Be grateful to the universe for having created a planet that contains everything you need.

- Be grateful for the beauty of the colors, textures and aromas of the vegetables, herbs or fruits, or a cup of coffee.

- Be grateful to the person who will share this meal with you.

- Be grateful that you can share your moment with that person and have each other's company.

- Be grateful that you have the ability to offer and share your meal.

- Be grateful that life is allowing this moment to sit, rest, replenish, keep each other's company and share whatever it is that needs to be shared at the moment.

By now, appreciation has started to flow from the heart and you will know if what you are about to eat is healthy for you. If you have to thank the chemicals named on the package that are so difficult to pronounce instead of the natural sweet aroma of a natural ripe tomato, you will know not to eat it. Your body will show you resistance. When appreciation flows from the heart, you will feel true comfort even when you drink plain water. Do it at your next meal. Do the same with your home, your family, your pet and your neighbor. Practicing heartfelt appreciation will change your perspective on life.

SELF-REALIZATION

"You have the power of pure energy within you to be, to do, to have, to accomplish, to become your dream." – Celina Tio

When you truly know your essence, everything changes easily. Your relationships are healthier by helping you grow with people who share your life's path. Life becomes pleasurable and enjoyable, and conflict and stress no longer emanate from you. You understand that ego makes peoples lives sad and full of problems, and that it drives competition, fear, war and destruction.

Knowing your essence also means the things that you're doing now are in line with what makes you feel happy. It's easy to identify if you're off balance because life no longer feels whole. You become aware of your energy and how it affects everything around you. You have a fresh understanding that you are part of creation, co-creating with all that makes us one.

You become more independent when you know your essence, investing into your wellbeing and happiness instead of things that have no value to your personal self. Rich and wealthy has a whole different meaning now. No more spending to do things or obtain things just because you feel bored or empty. You'll no longer feel the need to shop in an attempt to feel happy or, even worse, to look happy. You become independent and know that you are the only one responsible for how you are living your life, with no one else to blame. Vacationing to escape from reality is a thing of the past. Instead, you'll have the freedom to choose a destination that will give you enjoyment in everything from the planning to the adventure to the return.

At this point, inner peace has become real in your life and you'll have the self-realization that you truly are the creator of every moment in your life. Your future is right this moment, so make it amazing and wonderful. Move from the comfort spot of sameness, obedience and unhappiness. Walking on your self-pity will take you only to more of the same. It is time to tell yourself that you deserve to experience life, and to savor and indulge in the sweetness and pure love of creation. You deserve to feel free of unnecessary pain, have inner peace and feel truly loved.

Of course we all have sad moments in our lives. It is normal to experience loss and birth, laughter with tears of joy and also tears of sadness, and expansion and contraction. It is the Yin and Yang of life. What's important is what you do with it.

Your inner being has been waiting for you to listen truthfully to the pureness within. You are powerful beyond your comprehension, and have more than strength. You have the power of pure energy within you to be, to do, to have, to accomplish, and to become your dream. When I realized how powerful I was created to be, I stopped feeling small. I rid myself of unnecessary fears, choosing instead to be one with the moment. I learned to breathe moments out of love, peace and joy, and to share it with you and everyone around me. Let me help you heal. Allow me to guide you into that place of discovering and once and for all Honor Your Inner Treasures. Your life will be transformed.

www.honoryourinnertreasures.com

www.limitlessbeliefs.com

www.celinatioauthor.com

Family Is Everything

DAN ROGERS

Hundreds of years ago wooden ships brought immigrants to the shores of what would become the maritime provinces of Canada. Why did the pioneers brave starvation, malnutrition, disease or shipwreck?

Today, a number of immigrants arrived at Pearson International Airport in Toronto, Ontario. Why did they leave their countries, their jobs and friends to try and carve out a new life in Canada?

Ask such questions of either group and you would likely receive the identical answer: "To build a better life for my family," they would say. Why? Because family is everything!

In 1916 a young couple, Clarence and Lizzy, got married and boarded a train to northwest Saskatchewan. The rules were that if you were over eighteen, married and agreed to live on and work the land, the government would grant you a quarter section, which is 160 acres or 65 hectares.

At first they plowed the virgin fields with a team of oxen. The prairie grass roots were so thick that the girl had to follow along behind the plow, cutting the roots of the prairie grass with a butcher knife. Her first three babies miscarried. Then, on her fourth pregnancy, the boy rounded up just enough money for one train ticket to the closest town that had a hospital (Lloydminster). He took her in a horse drawn wagon across the prairie for many kilometers to the train station, put her on the train and returned home to continue working the fields. The girl gave birth to a healthy baby girl named Grace. That baby girl was my mother.

My grandmother was what was known as a Bernardo child. She was in a program based out of England that was founded by a man named Bernardo. Orphans and children whose parents could not afford to look after them were shipped to Canada to live on farms. Some of the families treated the child as one of their own, while others treated the child as a slave. The end result, however, was that they got to Canada. And it worked, albeit slowly. So … my mother had a better life than her mother … I am having a better life than my mother … and my son, an only child, came home from the hospital not only to his own bedroom, but to one that had a four piece en suite bathroom. Also, by the time my wife and I are gone from this world, he will be an automatic millionaire.

My hope is that you and your family can accomplish this quicker than we did. We were slow learners. It took us over a century to create wealth. But the fact that you are in Canada and reading this book already puts you in the group that is most likely to succeed. Do you find that hard to believe? Then just think of all the people who came home from work today and are either checking Facebook or watching reality TV. They definitely aren't reading a book about how to succeed financially.

THE PURPOSE OF THIS CHAPTER

The purpose of this chapter is to help educate you to use whatever money you have to benefit you and your family in the long run.

The first thing I want to do is ask you a question: What is your biggest asset? Many people will answer that question by stating what they own. Various answers will be the most obvious ones like my house, my car, my life insurance policy, my retirement fund. But the real answer is you or, to be more accurate, it's your ability to earn a living.

Now, consider that the average annual income in Canada is around fifty thousand dollars (at time of printing). That means in a typical forty year career you will have grossed two million dollars. Yet, most Canadians don't own two million dollars of mortgage free real estate or don't have two million dollars in the bank or even in an insurance policy. Why is that?

It's simple mathematics …

Mr. A and Mr. B both moved to Canada about fifty years ago from the same country. They both got jobs at the same company for the same wage. But Mr. A saved up his money for a down payment on a house and also budgeted in the monthly premium for a permanent life insurance policy, while Mr. B spent much of his disposable income on trips back to his homeland, coffee shops, take- out food, and cigarettes.

Both A and B died about twenty years ago. The daughter of Mr. A inherited a mortgage free house and a life insurance policy, while the son of Mr. B ended up with nothing. Because the child of A immediately had cash in hand, from the insurance money, and she chose to live in the house for free, she was able to invest both the life insurance money and the monthly rent she had previously been paying. Meanwhile, the son of Mr. B had to save for years and years before he could get out of the apartment he was renting, because saving up while paying rent is much more challenging. In the end, however, B descendent was able to buy a house and make some modest investments.

Eventually the heirs of both Mr. A and Mr. B died. The grandchildren of A have inherited multiple real estate properties and investment funds easily worth in excess of a million dollars, while the family of Mr. B ended up with only a few hundred thousand, as the real estate and other investments were purchased later in their parents' lives and didn't have time enough to grow. The property may not have even been mortgage free at the time of Mr. B's death.

So, the third generation of the A family are now millionaires, while the same generation of the B family has enough money for a modest down payment on a nice house.

You want to be Mr or Mrs A. Buy a home early and pay off that mortgage. Protect your ability to earn with the proper insurance policies and invest on an ongoing basis. Read on, I'll show you how to do it. But first a discussion about estate planning

WILL AND POWER OF ATTORNEY

We have been talking about estates. These are passed on to beneficiaries through the vehicle known as the will. But, over the several years that I have been in this profession, I have encountered a rather high percentage of people that do not have their wills done. And you do need one. Not a "do it yourself" will kit that can be purchased online or at a business supply retailer. Generally, the legal system does not consider this type of will to be valid. No, I strongly urge you to have a lawyer draw up your will. A good lawyer. A conscientious lawyer. Here's why …

An elderly widower sells his house, puts the money in the bank, moves to an apartment, and marries a much younger new wife. His lawyer draws up a will stating that his estate will be divided amongst his wife, his three children and his two favourite charities. The lawyer did not enquire about what type of account the money was in or ask any questions of that nature. When the man died, the executor of the estate found out that the bank had advised the man to name a beneficiary to the account, so the man, not being given a full legal explanation of the ramifications, named his wife as beneficiary. So, on his death, the bank immediately transferred 100% of the funds into the wife's name, and there was no legal recourse to get her to divide up the money according to the will. The will became a useless piece of paper. The three children and the two charities received nothing from the fund. That man was my father.

The lesson to be learned is to never assume that a professional you hire is automatically going to do things in your best interest.

Power of Attorney: There are two types of power of attorney: one for personal care, and one for property. This means that you designate a person to make decisions on your behalf should you reach the point where you can no longer make these decisions yourself. **Personal care** refers to topics such as choosing a personal support worker, a nursing home, treatments, medications, and other things of that nature. **Property** refers to topics such as whether or not to sell the house or rent it out or authorize repairs, and whether to sell the car, or cut the lawn or many other property related items.

In listing a power of attorney, remember that you do not have to have the same person for all areas. You could have a daughter who would be the best for personal care, an eldest son who would make the best executor, and a youngest son who is in real estate who would be the best person for property decisions.

I should also mention **Probate** as it is a complicated and frequently costly procedure wherein you must prove the validity of the will. The general rule is that if there is a beneficiary listed on the account, then probate is not required.

When the funds are in a bank, the money could be in one of several different types of accounts. It could be in a chequing account, a savings account, a TFSA (tax free savings account), an RRSP (registered retirement savings plan), mutual funds, segregated funds, GIC (guaranteed investment certificate), a RIF (retirement income fund), and a number of others. The bank would likely ask you to name a beneficiary on the account. This is done to prevent probate. However, remember the story about my father and learn from it. If there is only one person that you want to give your money to, then that is fine, but if there are multiple people, you must name them all.

PROTECT YOURSELF

In order to open this discussion, we need to go back to the reason everyone comes to Canada in the first place. We all know the answer to that one: to build a better life for your family. At the same time, we need to recall your greatest asset. It's you, and if you go down, everything that you worked for could be lost. So we are going to address a very important issue, income replacement. This is generally broken down into two areas; disability coverage and critical illness coverage.

Disability coverage: Disability insurance is meant to replace part of your income (usually 55%) in case of injury or illness. Now, the first thing to know is that not all disability policies are equal. Some give you the right see your own doctor—some do not. And that makes all the difference. The first group of claimants tends to be entrepreneurs who don't want to be away from their jobs any longer than the insurance company wants them to be. The second group of claimants tends to be more the corporate type, a type that encompasses malingerers—those people who are in no rush to get back to work after an injury or illness—the type that breeds distrust in the insurance companies. Make sure you're in the first group.

Integration of benefits: What this means is that if you signed up for a $2,000/month disability policy and you get hurt, and another organization also agrees to pay you let's say $1,200/month, whether it is another insurance company, Workers Safety Insurance Board, the employer, or whomever, then your insurance company only has to pay you the difference of $800/month. You can find policies that don't have this clause.

Return of Premium: What if you are lucky and never get injured? How would you like to get all your money back when you retire, tax free? Yes, there are disability policies available that have this benefit.

Soft tissue injuries/back injuries/sprains/strains: This is another very important feature. Many disability providers are so concerned about people faking injuries that they won't pay out unless something shows up on an X-ray. You don't want a policy like that. You want a policy that will cover you in all cases of injury or illness.

Injury occurs on or off the job: Many employers who provide a benefit plan to their employees will have disability coverage that only covers on the job accidents. While better than nothing, statistically, the average Canadian is more likely to get hurt in a car accident, at home, or while participating in sports and leisure than actually getting hurt on the job. That' the kind of coverage you want.

No limit on number of claims made: This one is fairly self-explanatory.

Make sure your provider does not have a clause where they can terminate your coverage if you make too many claims.

Critical Illness/Hospital Sickness Benefits: Let's imagine that you or your spouse were diagnosed with a terminal illness or a debilitating disease. The ill person might wish to do their "bucket list," go back to visit the homeland, see the Seven Wonders of the World, or take a cruise around the world. But from where would the money come? Cash in RRSPs? Sell the house? Remortgage the house? The problem with doing that is it ruins the whole game plan of coming to Canada to build a better life for your children and your children's children.

This is the reason that critical illness coverage exists in a place that already has state funded health care.

And just like disability coverage, it is possible to get critical illness coverage with a Return of Premium Clause, meaning that if you remain in good health, you get your money back at the end.

LIFE INSURANCE

There are many different types of life insurance. It is vitally important for you to know the differences so that you can pick the type that is the right one for your situation.

Reason for life insurance: Do you have massive debt from a mortgage or business loan that if all goes well you will have paid off before retirement? Or do you want to leave your family a lump sum of money for a particular purpose, regardless of whether you die young or old? These two situations require (differing) insurance products.

The standard formula that the insurance industry uses for determining the amount of coverage is: ten times annual salary plus debt. So if you make the average Canadian income of about $50,000 per year and have a three hundred thousand dollar mortgage, then the calculation would be to have $800,000 in coverage.

Term Insurance: Term insurance would be better understood by the public if it were renamed "temporary insurance." With term insurance you are buying a window of time. If you die in that window of time, the insurance company writes a cheque to your beneficiary. If you die outside that window, they cut no cheque at all.

Permanent insurance: Permanent insurance is frequently known by its official name, whole life insurance. If the reason for buying is that you need some security to pay off your debts if you die young, then term is the way to go, but if you want to leave a lump sum to your family whether you die next year or in sixty years, then you will want a permanent product.

Term to 100: Term to 100 is a rather unique type of life insurance that is sort of a hybrid between term insurance and permanent insurance. As we have already read, the disadvantage of a term policy is that it eventually runs out, but the advantage is lower premiums. The disadvantage of whole life coverage is that the premiums are high, but the advantage is that it lasts forever. What if you could get a policy that never runs out but that has the lower premiums more associated with term insurance? Great, right? That's why many companies don't offer the product. But you can find it, if that is what you want.

No Medical Insurance: No medical insurance is frequently called other names such as final expense insurance, funeral insurance, burial insurance, guaranteed issue insurance, instant issue insurance, and perhaps a few other names. It is frequently advertised by way of television commercials, and mail flyers delivered by the post office. The target client is often a retiree whose term insurance has now expired but who still wants to leave a lump sum when he or she dies. People with health problems who will never qualify for standard application coverage also tend to buy this type of policy.

Universal Life: This is another type of whole life policy. It can be a bit complicated, so I'm going to give a brief explanation of this product here. With a universal life policy, a portion of your premium goes into an investment. Over the years, the idea is for the investment to grow substantially. A universal life policy with a face amount of $100,000 would have an additional investment portion attached to it, so after a few decades the policy might pay out in total $150,000, $200,000 or more. Although this seems like a great idea, low interest rates over the past several years have made many people who hold a universal life policy realize that the projected payout at the end is going to be considerably lower than what the agent had suggested way back when the policy was first taken out.

The moral of this story is to make sure you sit down with a financial professional who will do a "needs analysis."

PLANNING FOR RETIREMENT

RRSP stands for Registered Retirement Savings Plan. An RRSP isn't an investment, it's a shell in which you can store all sorts of different kinds of financial plans and investments.

An RRSP could contain stocks, bonds, mutual funds, segregated funds, Guaranteed Investment Certificates, syndicate mortgages, Guaranteed Investment Accounts, just to name some of the more popular products that a typical Canadian RRSP might contain.

What an RRSP does is let you defer income tax. It is designed for Canadians who know that they are going to be bringing in less money after they retire than they are currently bringing in now. Canada Revenue Agency (CRA) charges income tax on a sliding scale depending on the income of the person. Someone who doesn't earn much income may pay no income tax at all, where someone with a high income might pay out 40% of their pay to income tax.

Life Income Fund: A life income fund generally comes from a company pension. Some employers offer a company matched retirement plan, meaning that whatever you put into it, they will contribute an equal amount. When you leave the company, it is recommended that you do something with it. The reason is that if the company runs into financial trouble, your retirement fund could be gone, or at least reduced. It has happened before, and will most likely happen again. Instead, if you quit, get downsized, or retire, you should move that money out of there and put it with an investment firm. That way, the success of your former employer will have no influence on the fund.

Various investments

Mutual funds are what are known as securities. The agent or broker must hold a license regulated by each provinces securities commission. Mutual funds are really just a collection of various stocks. They were designed for the purpose of the small investor being able to get into the stock market without a large cash outlay and with a lower risk. There are thousands of different funds out there, and virtually all of them are quite heavily diversified. This is both good news and bad news. The good news is that if one or a few of the companies that are inside that particular mutual fund take a huge nose dive, it won't cause your fund to drop too dramatically. The bad news is really the opposite side of the same coin. If a few of the stocks in the fund soar tremendously, your fund won't go up all that much because of all the other stocks in there that remain steadfast or have dropped. Mutual funds have no guarantees whatsoever, so if your fund dropped way down, you have only two choices: you can cash out at a loss, or you can hold onto it for enough years and hope that it rebounds satisfactorily. Mutual funds are also subject to fees known as Management Expense Ratios, or MER. If your fund's MER is 2%, then on a one hundred thousand dollar investment, expect to pay two thousand dollars per year in fees.

Segregated funds are very similar in concept to mutual funds. Segregated funds are sold by life insurance companies. Many financial experts describe segregated funds as "mutual funds with an insurance policy wrapper". Segregated funds must be kept separate from the insurance company's regular finances, hence the name. A "seg" fund and a mutual fund may both be investing in the same stocks, the main difference between the two, is there is a guarantee with a seg fund. The guarantee in a seg fund is generally either 75% or 100% of the original investment, depending on which plan you take. That means that you are guaranteed to get back either 75% or 100% of your money, even if the fund loses money. You will have to hold onto the fund for an agreed upon length of time, usually ten years to get this guarantee. And it is important to know that this guarantee is not free. A seg fund will have extra fees associated with it to cover this guarantee. If you cash out before the agreed upon time, you get what is in the fund, whether it has gained money or lost money, less any fees. If the seg fund rises in value, most plans will allow you to "reset" the guaranteed amount to this higher amount, however, that would mean that doing this will reset the amount of time, usually ten years, that you must hold the fund.

Depending on which plan you take, 75% or 100%, if you die while the funds are down, your beneficiary will receive 75% or 100% of the fund.

Guaranteed Investment Certificate (GIC): A GIC is a savings account where the interest rate is pre-set. There is an amount of time, generally two years, three years, four years, or five years that you must keep the money in the account in order to obtain that interest rate. If you withdraw the funds earlier than that date, you won't get the agreed upon interest rate. The longer you keep the money locked up, the higher the interest rate you can get.

Guaranteed Investment Account (GIA): The simplest way to describe a GIA is that it is like a GIC, except it is carried by insurance companies, just like seg funds, and the guarantee activates in the event of the contract holder's death.

If the contract holder dies while having a GIA, the company guarantees the highest of the two following things: either the balance of the account on the date of death; or 100% of the sum invested in this account.

Syndicated Mortgages: A developer who wants to build a condo tower, a commercial office building, or any other large construction project can generally only get conventional bank financing up to a certain percentage of the cost of the project. The remainder of the amount he needs has to come from someplace else. When you agree to give the developer your money, you go on title, the same way that your bank is on title for your house, if you have a mortgage. Syndicated mortgages have been around for a long time, but ordinary folk like you and me have only started hearing about them in the past few years. The reason is that they used to be reserved for those with very large sums to invest, like a million dollars. It was only relatively recently that the industry opened up the market dramatically by lowering the minimum investment to twenty five thousand dollars. Generally, the syndicate mortgages that have come across my desk pay 8% per annum, simple interest. It is important to know the difference between simple interest and compound interest. With compound interest, you receive interest on your interest, but with simple interest you do not. A typical syndicate mortgage locks your money away for a period of time, frequently three or four years.

Gold and other precious metals: The only reason that I am even mentioning this topic is because I am told that there are people on the radio urging us to buy gold. On the financial security pyramid or pillars, or ladder, or however you would like to refer to it, precious metals are to be considered at the top, right up there with collecting works of art. This means that it is something that would be recommended to do after your house is mortgage free, and you have amassed considerable wealth and assets.

REAL ESTATE

Buy vs Rent: There are always those who debate whether or not it is better to rent and invest more in the market, or buy real estate, and subsequently have less money left over at the end of the month to invest. Remember that home ownership has two entirely separate goals. The first one is to make money on it, either by buying low and selling high, or by making improvements to the property, thus increasing its value, or by paying off the mortgage so that you no longer have the expense of making payments. The second goal is to improve your quality of life. You have your very own residence without being at the mercy of a landlord, should they decide to sell the property, or raise the rent, or move into it themselves, or move a relative into it. You also have total control over what colour you would like the walls painted, the types of light fixtures, window coverings, faucets, countertops, and a host of other features.

Buying Real Estate: The first thing you will require is the **minimum down payment**. When you buy with less than twenty percent down, this is what the banks refer to as a high ratio mortgage. This requires you to have mortgage default insurance. The most popular organization the banks use to obtain mortgage default insurance is the Canada Mortgage and Housing Corporation (CMHC), a crown corporation. Two other companies that offer this are Genworth Financial Canada, and Canada Guaranty. They will charge a fee, and blend it into your payment. This can only be avoided by having a minimum of twenty percent of the purchase price of the property already saved up and available. For a first time home buyer, this could be difficult. Most of the property purchases I have made had CMHC on them. I still found this to be the lesser of the evils when compared to paying rent.

Next, you will need to **obtain approval for the mortgage**. You should do this before looking at any properties. There are two ways of doing this. The first is to talk to your own bank branch. The second is to use a mortgage broker. The advantage of using a mortgage broker is twofold. First, they do all the work, don't charge you and get paid a referral fee from the financial institution where the mortgage is placed. The second advantage is that they will frequently work with multiple lenders, giving them and you more choices. One thing they will be looking for is your Total Debt Service Ratio (TDSR). This means that all your payments, mortgage, utilities, and other things such as car loan payments and line of credit payments should not exceed approximately forty percent of your overall gross household income. So first of all, you should not be considering real estate if you owe any money on anything else, and yes, that includes your car.

The next thing is your need to have established a **credit rating**. There are two credit rating services. The most popular one is Equifax, and the other one is TransUnion. You can obtain your credit score from these institutions yourself at no charge. They will probably try to get you to pay for it, and they will quite likely offer you the information instantly if you pay, but you can wait and get it the slow way without having to pay. If you are new to the country, or young, or both, you may not have established a credit rating. The first thing is to have a credit card. Obviously, the intended goal is to pay the balance off every statement, thus avoiding any interest payments. If you think you can get by in this world without a credit card, you thought wrong. Not only is it vital in establishing a credit rating, but without one, it is generally quite difficult to purchase anything online, obtain tickets for a major event, rent a car, book a flight, stay in a hotel, and a host of various other situations that will cross your path from time to time.

Types of properties: There are really only four: condo, townhouse, semi, and detached

Condo is short for condominium. You will usually see them in the form of high rise buildings, but there are townhouse condos and even detached condos. With a condo you only own the inside, the condo corporation owns the outside. I'm using simple terminology here. You pay a monthly fee to them and they are responsible for exterior things like the roof, landscaping, snow removal, elevators, and really everything this is not inside your unit.

The next type of property on the scale is the **townhouse**. They can be condos or freehold. If it is a townhouse condo, you pay a fee to the condo corporation, just like a high rise, and they look after the same things like the roof, snow removal, and grass cutting. If it is a freehold, you own the whole thing, and you are responsible for everything. The main items to think about with a townhouse is that you share your walls with someone else.

Next on the list is the **semi-detached**. This has all the same possible downsides as a townhouse, but you are only sharing one wall. The key to a good semi is to have a great neighbour on the other side of the wall. But of course, you have very little way of finding that out until you are already moved in.

A **detached house**, meaning that it is not connected to any other building (you can walk all the way around all four sides), is the ultimate goal, in my humble opinion. In many regions, especially in the Greater Toronto Area (GTA), the detached house is sought after not only for the buffer zone between neighbours, but because many of these houses are ideally suited to having a separate basement apartment with a separate entrance, frequently a side door. This is an excellent way to bring in extra money to offset the high mortgage payment.

GOVERNMENT RETIREMENT BENEFITS

There are five main areas about which you will need to know: Canada Pension Plan (CPP), Canada Pension Plan Survivor Benefit, Canada Pension Plan Death Benefit, Old Age Security (OAS) and Guaranteed Income Supplement (GIS).

The Canada Pension Plan (CPP) is something that you would have paid into during the course of your working career. You can apply for it as early as age sixty or as late as age seventy. If you apply for it at age sixty, you will, however, receive a 36% reduction in benefits. If you apply for it at age seventy, you will get an increase of 42%.

According to the government of Canada statistics as of the year 2015, the average CPP monthly benefit is $619 and the maximum is $1,065.

Old Age Security: The Old Age Security (OAS) is a benefit for which you can apply at age sixty five, as of now, however, there are plans to increase the age at which you can apply to age sixty seven. Time will tell if the federal government sticks to the plan of age sixty seven, or if successive governments decide to roll it back to age sixty five. At time of publishing, the OAS is around $565 per month, however, it is indexed to inflation, so it generally goes up a few dollars per month every year.

CPP Survivor Benefit: If you are the first to die in a spousal or common-law relationship, the surviving spouse should apply for this benefit. It is generally 60% of the deceased partner's monthly CPP benefit, or if death occurs before age sixty five, then this benefit is calculated on the amount that it would have been if death had occurred at age sixty five.

CPP Death Benefit: Only a very few countries offer this benefit. To be eligible for your estate to receive this benefit you must have made contributions to CPP in the lesser of: one third of the calendar years in your CPP contributory period, but no less than three calendar years; or ten calendar years.

The amount of the death benefit depends on how much and for how long the deceased contributed to the CPP. The maximum benefit is $2,500. According to the latest statistics, the average benefit is around $2,300. The CPP death benefit is calculated as the amount equal to six months' worth of your monthly CPP benefit.

Guaranteed Income Supplement (GIS): If you live in Canada and have a low income, this monthly non-taxable benefit can be added to your Old Age Security (OAS) pension, if your annual income (or in case of a couple, your combined income) is less than the maximum annual income. The Canadian government calculates this maximum annual income amount based on numerous different criteria such as if you are single, widowed, or divorced, or if you have a spouse that receives the full OAS pension, or if your spouse does not receive the OAS, or if your spouse is already receiving the GIS and the

OAS. You can always go the government's website yourself when you need this information: www.servicecanada.gc.ca

FINAL ARRANGEMENTS

This section will be dealing with an area that most people are not particularly thrilled about discussing. Furthermore, most people are not willing to walk into a funeral home and ask questions. Fortunately, I worked in the industry for ten years, so I'm in the position to not only help you spare your family a lot of grief and hardship, but at the same time, save you money as well.

There are two ways to pre-arrange your funeral: One way is to pre-arrange but not pre-pay. The other, and more preferred way, is to pre-arrange and pre-pay.

Cremation verses Burial: The main reason that 90 % of the people I have talked to about funerals over the years choose cremation, is so they can avoid the cemetery completely.

If you choose cremation, there are five options open to you regarding the disposition of the remains.

1. Your family can take the urn home with them and put it on the shelf. (This is not for everyone, some like the idea, some hate it.)

2. You can have the ashes scattered. Note: this choice is completely legal.

3. If you have an immediate family member that is already in a cemetery plot, most cemetery boards will allow you to place your urn in your family member's plot, generally for a fee of a few hundred dollars.

4. You can purchase your very own plot and have your urn buried there.

5. Cemeteries have structures called columbariums, or wall niches, that you can purchase for the purpose of having your urn placed there permanently.

Funeral Service Choices: For the sake of simplicity, there are really only three.

1. **A Direct Disposition.** All this means is that you are hiring the services of a licensed funeral director to send a transfer vehicle to your place of death, whether that is a hospital, a nursing home, or your own home. They will pick up the remains and transport them back to the preparation room at the funeral home, arrange for the cremation and return the ashes to you.

2. **A Memorial Service** contains everything a direct disposition contains, but the funeral establishment puts on a service, either in their own building, or in the church of your choice. Sometimes people want it to be held in a different location, such as a club that has their own facilities. It is important to note that with a memorial service, the body is not present, no casket is present, cremation has already taken place, and most often, the urn is present in lieu of a casket.

3. **A Traditional Service**: This is the type of arrangement where the casket is present. I'm not sure why, but many people are under the misconception that a traditional service is not available with cremation. The facts are that there are only two real differences between a traditional service with cremation to follow, and a traditional service with burial to follow. The first difference is that with burial, there is a funeral procession from the funeral home or church to the cemetery, and with cremation to follow, there is not, because the body has to be transported to the crematorium. The second difference is that with burial, a casket

is purchased, and the casket is buried. But with cremation, the funeral home usually provides the use of the casket for the visitation and service, and hidden inside the casket underneath the white satin lining, where no one can see, is the combustible, rigid, leak-proof container that is always necessary with cremation.

"I'm donating my body to science!"

This is what you need to know with regards to whole body donation. Medical schools, or schools of anatomy will accept body donations to train future medical professionals. It is completely different than donating organs. The body must be in very good condition and there must be a need for the body. It is important to remember that if you have a pre-paid funeral and you are accepted by a medical school, the pre-paid funeral fund will be returned to the family with interest.

SUMMARY

What do all of these things I've been talking about have in common? The greatest point of all that I've written here is that there are many ways for you to achieve wealth and grow it. An early mortgage and long-term investments can result in a free home for your loved ones to live in, money for them to live on and funds to grow even more money. They can even take the money they used to pay rent with and purchase yet more investments, so that when the third generation matures, there is a literal fortune waiting for them to inherit.

We also discussed investment vehicles such as real estate, mutual funds and term deposits, touching on various types of each, the idea being to make you aware of the choices you have moving forward. We even talked about how to protect your earning potential with disability insurance and life insurance. The chapter ended with a looked at funeral planning.

You came to Canada to make a better life for your family. This chapter can set you on the proper path to achieve what you wish. Good luck in all you do!

The Get-Back-Up Revolution

Overcome Depression, Failure
and Fear in 10 Simple Steps

JEAN KOR

Failures, broken relationships, illnesses, deaths of loved ones, injuries, lost moments of greatness, or sometimes just sheer stupidity, occur in our lives at one point or another. We have all had times when we doubt ourselves, when our fear keeps us from daring to follow our heart's desire. There are days when everything seems to go wrong, when we make mistakes and feel like hiding from the world.

There are days, too, when it is even hard to get out of bed, let alone do something that needs to get done. Worse still, when we sit in these feelings for too long, we fall into a downward spiral of despair, hopelessness and depression.

Professional help is always an option but, all too often, that leads to medication. If you are like me, you would much rather find a solution that does not involve prescription drugs or years of therapy. Plus, many of these negative emotions are often based on real life problems that require you to "snap out of it," immediately, and on your own.

Sometimes things that happen to you may seem horrible, unfair and painful at first. If you take a step back, you will see that it is through these challenging times that you are able to find strength, courage, beauty and love in yourself and your surroundings in the most unexpected ways.

Believe me, I know. At one point in my life, I was overwhelmed by fear and despair. I was living as two people. Privately, I was an emotional wreck, fearful, lonely and depressed. I was struggling to save my marriage. My grandma died after a long illness that began with a stroke, and immediately afterwards my mum was diagnosed with cancer. The thought of losing her, my husband and more loved ones further consumed me. I regretted my migration to Canada, and regretted the fact that I did not spend more time with my family.

To make matters worse, my finances suffered, and I misjudged several important decisions. I was broken — I felt like a failure as a daughter, a wife and a leader of my sisters. I hated myself, my life and everything that was happening to me. Publicly, I was the rock on which my family could depend. Quietly, I cried alone for many nights.

THE CHAOS OF MY MIND

I kept telling myself, "All this is beyond my control. There's nothing that I can do. I am so pitiful. I am such a loser." All the while, the dialogue in my head was so negative.

When you keep telling yourself the same story over and over again, you end up believing it. *Instead of finding solutions, I was looking for people and things to blame.* I was stuck in a negative, unproductive place and could not find the light. I isolated myself from my friends and my family, and further spiraled into a deeper state of depression.

Staying in a negative place is unhealthy; not just emotionally, but physically. My health deteriorated. The doctors were puzzled. Multiple tests, heart exams and MRI's showed no major medical problems. It was stress and depression that were causing all my ailments. I could feel myself rotting away in despair. I hated how I felt. I wanted my life to improve, but I didn't know how to make the change. In my mind, my problems were insurmountable. They were unsolvable puzzles with no possible solutions.

I craved something more, something better, but just didn't know how to tone down 'the negative voices' I heard constantly and find the positive shift I needed. I didn't know where to start. Then, I realized that I was the only one holding the missing pieces of the jigsaw puzzle I was trying to solve. I was always waiting for a divine intervention, a miracle and someone to help me solve my problems. *Instead of always seeking external advice and approval, what I actually needed was to decide take charge of my life and help myself up on my feet.*

SNAPPING OUT OF IT!

One night, dwelling in self-pity and loneliness, I thought, "I don't want to feel sad tonight; I am just too exhausted for this. I need to snap out of it!" In that instant, I remembered being a kid and playing with an inflatable roly-poly toy filled with sand at the base. I remembered punching it and wrestling it to the ground but, regardless of how hard I tried to keep it down, the toy would always bounce back up to its feet. I thought how nice it would be if I had one of those with me at the moment.

That night, I had a purpose. I decided to make one of those toys to cheer myself up. Immediately, my focus changed, and I forgot about my problems. I started looking for ways to make the toy. I took out my sewing machine, cut up an old t-shirt, took stuffing from a pillow, and made myself a roly-poly bunny — truth be told, a pretty crummy looking bunny filled with rice at the base. But ...It was soft and comforting. I pushed it down, and it immediately got back up on its feet, and that put a big smile on my face. It was exactly as I remembered.

Then I drew a zany expression with squinty eyes on the blank bunny's face. I wanted the face to represent life's journey. The squiggly mouth I drew meant that life was full of ups and downs. The fact that the smile ended in an upturn meant that, despite all the challenges, life would end with an upward victory smile!

"Stay strong, bunny! Get back on your feet and never give up!" I spoke out loud to the bunny, but it wasn't the bunny that needed to hear those words. I needed the positive words of encouragement.

Now, the crummy looking bunny I made wasn't invincible. After several falls, it got stuck in an awkward position and couldn't get back up on its feet. However, when I gave it a little nudge, it quickly bounced back up again. It reminded me of the many times when I had hard times, made mistakes or felt like a failure and my family and friends were always there to love me unconditionally, and help me up on my feet again.

When I looked at my bunny, I saw *perseverance, strength, positivity, gratitude, love* and *support*. It felt alive and real. I was so excited by my discovery that the resilient bunny I had created could help me feel so much better so quickly. He could be knocked down, but he always got back up, just like what I needed to do.

I quickly shot a video of my bunny and immediately shared it with my family and friends. They all loved it! Everyone wanted one as it resonated with the daily struggles they all had in their lives. It soon got the nickname the *NEVER GIVE UP BUNNY* because of the symbolic message of resiliency it demonstrates.

A DECISION TO SHIFT MY FOCUS

I knew then that I couldn't change the things that had happened, but I could change how I felt in any given moment.

I wanted to be happy.

I wanted to have a happy relationship.

I wanted to be fit and healthy again.

I wanted to make my parents happy.

I wanted to be successful.

I wanted to be someone that my siblings looked up to.

I wanted to be able to cheer my family up and improve their lives.

I knew I must make a change in order to be happy. I resolved to change my attitude first. By shifting to positive questions, focusing on what I wanted (and not what I hated), *I started to find solutions to get the results I craved.* Before, my problems were huge, unsolvable puzzles. Now I know that I don't need to wait for all the answers to overcome my problems. Instead of being overwhelmed, I can just start by taking one tiny step at a time. By breaking down a problem into a series of small achievable tasks, I can then easily tackle each task until I achieve all the goals I have set. That shift in approaching a problem would change how I felt about finding a solution.

HELPING OTHERS

I wanted my family and friends to have the same feeling of comfort and confidence that I had found in my zany *NEVER GIVE UP BUNNY*. During my darkest moments, my bunny helped me find the courage to pick myself up, dust myself off and get 'hopping' once again.

Over the next few months I looked back at my struggles and journey and came up with a ten step plan for overcoming depression, failure, lack of motivation, fear and self-doubt. These steps will help propel you into a world where answers can be found in difficult situations and trying times.

Step 1: Get Serious and Decide — Do You Want Things to Change?

If you don't like your current situation, then decide that you really want it to change and *get serious* about it! Only you have the power to make that decision. *"For things to change, first you have to change."* Change sounds scary, but, if you want new results you have to be willing to give it a go. If you keep doing what you have been doing, you will keep getting what you have been getting. I understand that most of us are fearful of change because of the uncertainties that lie ahead. Don't be scared!

Step 2: Take a Timeout – Stop Complaining and Be Thankful

Stop the negative inner dialogue. Don't be preoccupied with hating everything around you, complaining about everything and thinking that everything is going against you. You need room to see, feel, realize and receive the good things happening around you. Some of us would find ways to 'dislike' every good thing and believe that it was, indeed, a negative. When you focus on what you hate or dislike, that is exactly what you are going to get. *Remember that you are only as pathetic as you believe yourself to be.*

Emotional hurts don't last unless you hang on to them. Don't let harsh words linger in your mind creating a negative dialogue that gets bigger as you repeat it and dwell on it.

Be thankful. Take a moment to stop and think about all the good things that have happened to you. As dire as things may seem at the moment, dig deep and find the littlest thing that you can be thankful for. I created a gratitude journal. I started with being thankful for a blessed life, an able body, having a roof above my head, food on the table, great friends and family who love me. Then I started seeing beauty in the little things I took for granted. I became thankful for the smiling cashier, a chat with friends over coffee, the smooth traffic and the extra nut I found on my banana nut muffin.

Step 3: Tell Yourself You Deserve to Be Happy

Eventually, your inner dialogue will change. You will understand that you are valuable and deserve all the positive changes happening in your life. God made everyone equal and does not discriminate. Regardless of whom you are, what your background is, or what your past was, the only thing that matters is the present and what you do to create a better tomorrow.

Oprah Winfrey said, *"Change is possible. Greatness is possible. But you can't do anything unless you first believe in yourself.*" So, hold your head up high because you have every right to do so. Tell yourself you are a special person and a great individual. Believe in yourself, because if you don't, no one else will. Start by writing down 50-100 reasons why you deserve all the good things in life and why you love yourself. Include your strengths, skills and good qualities. You do not have to be shy or humble in this exercise. Go ahead — compliment, praise and love yourself for any reason.

Step 4: Take Responsibility for Your Own Life

It is easier to find excuses, dodge the issues and always put the blame on others. By doing so, we leave our lives in other people's hands — always playing the helpless victim, waiting and hoping for help that may never come. In order to take charge of our lives and destiny, we need to be self-reliant and understand that nobody owes us anything. You have to be responsible for your own needs, emotions, physical well-being, economic, social and spiritual. Stop figuring out why and how you fell into the hole you are in. Instead, start thinking about how to get out. Stop waiting for help. Help yourself. You have to take action.

Step 5: Set Your Goals, Be Clear About What You Want

Clarity is power. The clearer the reason for change, the easier it will be to accomplish your goal. Ask yourself: "Why do I want to change?" Associate the end goal with all the pleasure and possible delightful results. Consider all the pain, suffering and negative consequences of staying where you are. Let these immense visualizations be your driving force. You need to understand, change is never a matter of ability. It is a matter of motivation, of having the desire to create that change.

Set your goals; break them down into simple, small and achievable tasks. Work on a plan to become more organized and tackle the tasks you have been avoiding. Having a goal to work on gives you a sense of purpose and, just by working on it, you will immediately feel happier.

Step 6: Get the Tools and Take Action

Knowing what you want to change, and why you want to change is just the first step in creating that positive change. *You have to take action. Not just small action but MASSIVE, EARTH SHATTERING ACTION!* Equip yourself with the right "tools" to achieve your goals and attain the results that you want.

Go back to school, get a treadmill, get more training and invest in yourself. If you find that the tool you have is not producing the results.

Step 7: Change Your Inner Dialogue

You have the goals, you understand the reasons, and you have the tools. Why have you not followed through? You may have hit a small obstacle. Your inner demon may be talking to you. It's saying, "I knew this would not work." You believe it because that is the conversation you have had with yourself for years. *Stop it!* You can do this. Change your perspective and tackle that obstacle. Instead of focusing on the problem, focus on the solutions. If you keep telling yourself that change is good and that you can do it, eventually you will believe it.

Step 8: Conquer your Fear

Everybody is afraid. Have you ever ridden a rollercoaster? The reason why it is so exciting is because you are testing the limits of what is safe. People who design roller coasters have found a way to use fear and turn it into a thrilling experience. You need to find a *way to use your fear to propel you into action* instead of

letting it destroy you. Don't pretend that fear is not there. Challenge yourself. If you are afraid, ask yourself, "Will a negative result be worse than doing nothing and maintaining the status quo?" Focus on what you want, not what you are afraid of. Change your inner dialogue.

Step 9: Anticipate Challenges & Reward Yourself

Life is not a straight path. Anticipate that there will be ups and downs along the way, and don't be overly stressed when you hit a bump on the road. There are many forks in the road. Look at the possible outcomes and evaluate them. There will be challenges and road blocks, and you might even make the wrong turn occasionally, but that is as anticipated. Admit it. Then change it. Every wrong turn brings you closer to your destination as long as you keep on going and don't give up. In knowing this, you will be calm in the face of adversity. Remember to celebrate and reward yourself for your actions and successes. You are your greatest critic or your loudest cheerleader. Be a cheerleader!

Step 10: Create and Maintain a Strong Positive Foundation

For anything to grow, it must have a strong foundation and a robust environment. Create and cultivate a group of people who love and support you. Find people who challenge you to be better, and encourage you to try new solutions. Find workshops that add new tools to your toolkit. Keep expanding your expectations. Last but not least, taking care of the health of our minds and bodies is fundamental for ensuring that we will have the energy and vitality to create the life we want. For me, the moment I decided to take responsibility for my own life and not let depression consume me, I felt powerful, alive and free from the shackles in which I had bound myself. Having long-term goals to work on gives me a purpose and helps me grow each day. I have started a blog sharing fun and inspirational materials as well as the zany looking bunny which was, and still is, my source of strength and a constant reminder of perseverance.

It has not been smooth sailing. Trust me, there were many, many times when I struggled hard and just wanted to give up. It certainly was not easy, but I am glad that I found the strength to get back up on my feet and make a positive difference in this world.

You may never know exactly what tomorrow holds for you, but for now, smile through your tears, laugh at the confusion, wink at the fear, and remind yourself to stay strong always. Never ever give up. Pick yourself up, create the life you deserve and live life with absolutely no regrets.

If you know someone who could use a *NEVER GIVE UP BUNNY* or want to share your personal journey with me, please visit www.nevergiveupbunny.com.

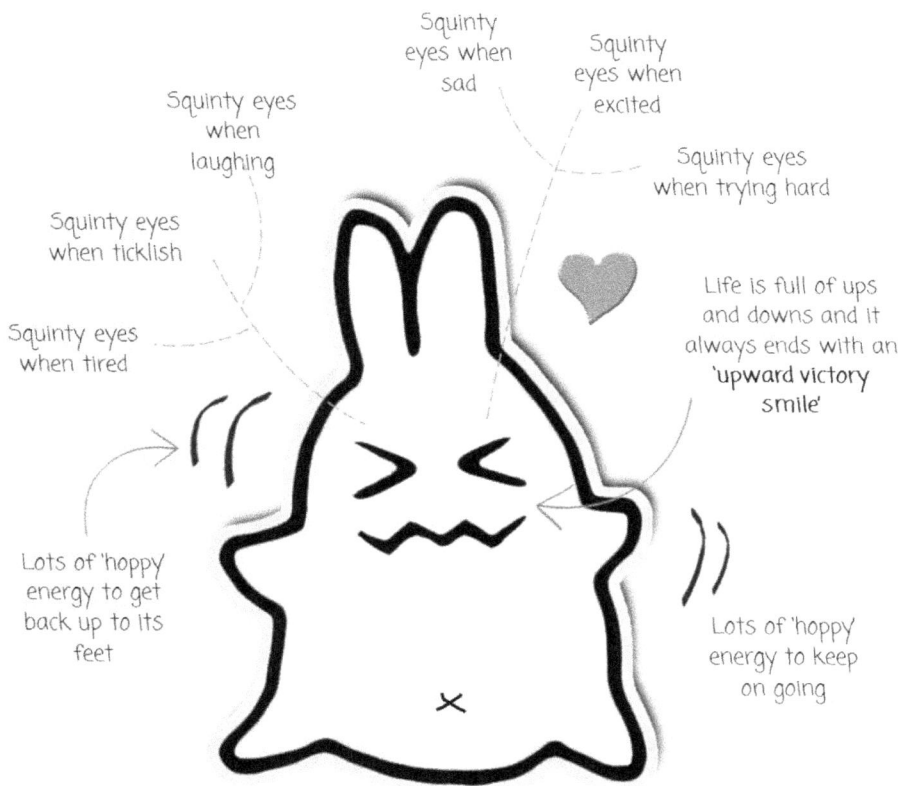

Squinty eyes when sad

Squinty eyes when excited

Squinty eyes when laughing

Squinty eyes when trying hard

Squinty eyes when ticklish

Squinty eyes when tired

Life is full of ups and downs and it always ends with an 'upward victory smile'

Lots of 'hoppy' energy to get back up to its feet

Lots of 'hoppy' energy to keep on going

Anatomy of a NEVER GIVE UP BUNNY

www.ingramcontent.com/pod-product-compliance
Lightning Source LLC
Chambersburg PA
CBHW052043090426

42739CB00010B/2030